Men-at-Arms • 561

Ground Forces in the Korean War 1950–53 (2)

The US Army and US Marine Corps

Robert C. Mackowiak • Illustrated by Johnny Shumate

Series editors Martin Windrow & Nick Reynolds

OSPREY PUBLISHING

Bloomsbury Publishing Plc

Kemp House, Chawley Park, Cumnor Hill, Oxford OX2 9PH, UK

29 Earlsfort Terrace, Dublin 2, Ireland

1385 Broadway, 5th Floor, New York, NY 10018, USA

E-mail: info@ospreypublishing.com

www.ospreypublishing.com

OSPREY is a trademark of Osprey Publishing Ltd

First published in Great Britain in 2025

A catalog record for this book is available from the British Library.

ISBN: PB 9781472862648; eBook 9781472862655; ePDF 9781472862662; XML 9781472862631

25 26 27 28 29   10 9 8 7 6 5 4 3 2 1

Index by Rob Munro

Typeset by PDQ Digital Media Solutions, Bungay, UK

Printed by Repro India Ltd.

MIX
Paper
FSC FSC® C047271

Osprey Publishing supports the Woodland Trust, the UK's leading woodland conservation charity.

To find out more about our authors and books visit **www.ospreypublishing. com**. Here you will find extracts, author interviews, details of forthcoming events and the option to sign up for our newsletter.

Title-page photograph: Men receiving awards illustrate the vast array of colors, patterns, and wear to the HBT uniform. HBT jackets variously feature box pockets, pleated pockets, and small patch pockets. It is possible that the officer closest to the camera and fourth man in might wear M1945 HBT trousers, but all the others wear cargo-pocket types. Note also the use of unit and rank insignia on uniform and helmets. The Marines still practiced clasping the chinstrap properly or allowed it to dangle loosely, but within the Army, the custom of wearing the canvas chinstrap of the shell around the back rim of the helmet prevailed as a mythical carryover from World War II. Though they had no hard evidence, troops firmly believed that any explosion to their front would catch the helmet with such force it would decapitate them or at least break their neck – a severe exaggeration that almost every soldier firmly believed. The advantage to this practice, in reality, was that the common soldier frequently took his helmet off to use for anything other than head protection, especially for a quick seat, so clasping and unclasping the chinstrap became an inconvenience. (Author's Collection)

GROUND FORCES IN THE KOREAN WAR 1950–53 (2)

THE US ARMY AND US MARINE CORPS

INTRODUCTION

The outbreak of the Korean War caused a hasty scramble for US units in Japan to reorganize and deploy to the Korean peninsula as rapidly as possible. Initially, the assumption was that any North Koreans would simply flee at the sight of American troops. Unfortunately, this brazen mindset doomed the initial deployments of troops who were provided entirely with outdated surplus equipment or not equipped properly at all. Soldiers and Marines alike suffered until it became clear that the war in Korea would be a horribly drawn-out affair.

Marines wearing a mixture of "boondockers" (service shoes) with leggings and double-buckle boots. Of the three nearest to camera, the Marine on left has his P1944 trousers rolled up over his leggings; the Marine center also wears boondockers with leggings, but has his P1944 trousers tucked in; and the Marine to the right wears buckle boots. Note also their bare helmets with unbuckled chinstraps (except for the Marine in center), soft cap worn under the helmet, stenciled rank on the uniform (corporal center and platoon sergeant very faintly on right), and the clear depiction of field gear including a poncho or similar piece folded over the belt of the Marine in center. (US Navy Medicine Photo #09-7966-009)

Two types of World War II-surplus "Jacket, Herringbone Twill" worn during the Korean War show both pleat pocket and box pockets, the retained gas flap, and 13-star buttons. The corporal chevrons of old stock and M1951 sergeant first class chevrons display the use of rank insignia on the field jackets. (Author's Collection)

THE BASICS

Herringbone Twill: Army

Beginning in the brutal summer of 1950, the typical Army combat soldier arrived in Korea wearing the basic herringbone twill (HBT) field uniform of World War II vintage with large cargo pockets on the chest and hips. Some of the newer, cleaner cut and less baggy 1947-pattern uniforms found a way into the supply stream, but these were not dominant until 1951. Typical underwear was white, not olive drab, and undershirts were T-shirt cut.

First appearing in 1941 and subsequently issued in simplified and improved variants, the HBT fatigues were intended to be worn over "wools" as a coverall type of outer garment, but were quickly adopted as a standalone combat uniform that wore extremely well in hard conditions. While HBT outlasted most other materials, tears in the material came quickly to the knees, pocket corners, hems, and collars. Cuffs of the baggy sleeves were often turned back to keep them from falling over the hands. In the initial days of fighting, it was common to see the HBT jacket worn untucked, but very quickly the single most significant change in how the jacket was worn came when soldiers began to tuck it into their trousers.

All patterns of the Army "Jacket, Herringbone Twill" and "Trousers, Herringbone Twill" were issued and worn in Korea, including those appended with the term "Special," which featured a gas flap (frequently cut out) inside the button front. This design featured two large chest pockets that extended to the abdomen and could comfortably hold a K-ration box. These jackets were first produced with metal 13-star buttons but many later examples substituted sewn-on plastic buttons. Both box pockets and pleated pockets appear as well. This pattern (with all of its own varieties) was the most widely issued until the revised type "Jacket, Herringbone Twill, Olive Drab Shade 7" and "Trousers, Herringbone Twill, Olive Drab Shade 7" entered the supply chain during World War II.

The OD No. 7 type was a further simplification of the uniform set. The gas flap was omitted, pockets were made smaller, and the trousers were redesigned with front and rear patch pockets rather than the pair of cargo pockets. It was generally less baggy and loose fitting than the World War II patterns, and sizes were revised from numerical measurements to small, medium, and large.

The M1941 HBT jacket was the least common in Korea, and the matching trousers were not likely to have made it into the supply chain at all. The author has observed the early-pattern jacket to be issued to soldiers requiring unusually large sizes, so it may be that they only remained in supply to fulfill such needs.

From the beginning of the Korean War, the HBT uniform was worn just as frequently with and without insignia. Officers displayed their metal collar insignia and enlisted men their rank insignia sewn on the sleeves. Unit patches and qualification badges were also common. Watches, whistle chains, and other personal items were often fixed through the lapel buttonhole. Further modifications later in the Korean War made affordances for additional personal items. Added shoulder loops provided a space for regimental insignia and officers' rank insignia. Even if these were not worn, the added shoulder loops created a more military appearance and were a popular addition. Sleeve pockets often consisted of one "cigarette pocket" type, a basic patch pocket aptly named as it was appropriately sized for a typical package of cigarettes, on one sleeve. On the other sleeve, a similarly sized but partitioned pocket, sometimes with loops above, became the "pen pocket" to hold pens, pencils, spoons, and pipes. When added to worn and faded uniforms, newer olive-drab material against faded sage showed a stark contrast of uneven wear.

Trousers were most commonly tucked into cuffed two-buckle boots or lace-up combat boots. In the early days of the war this practice was strictly

An excellent example of what became the standard HBT jacket in Korea is the 1947-type jacket with applied sleeve pockets, simple nametape, and full-color unit patch. (Author's Collection)

These three pairs of trousers show material difference across different uniform types, but by the Korean War period all were produced in a similar style. From left to right: the M1943 trousers in OD No. 7, simplified 1947-type HBT trousers, and OD33-shade wool trousers. (Author's Collection)

A lieutenant wears HBT coveralls in the field. Note his helmet cover and M1948 boots. (Author's Collection)

functional and not done for presentation. Less presentable but frequently done was simply rolling up the cuff of the trouser leg to hang over the boot.

The one-piece coverall suit was also a popular choice of garment for the front-line soldier. Intended for mechanics and other personnel the nature of whose work was likely to soil uniforms, the simple uniform was also oversized with an integral cloth belt, a single small patch pocket on the chest, and similar hip and rear pockets with flaps. The coverall was used sparingly by front-line troops, but certainly made an appearance in the field outside of workshops and hangars.

Herringbone Twill: Marine

The Marines wore both P1941 and P1944 HBT utility sets that were even less distinguishable from their World War II counterparts than the Army's by comparison. The Marine Corps still utilized khaki canvas leggings as part of their field uniform ensemble, something that was dropped by the Army at the end of World War II. The Marine Corps' load-carrying equipment, denoted "782" gear, included the P1941 pack system, jungle first-aid kit, and a pair of canteens often with the distinctive cross-flap carrier, which was all exclusive to the Marine Corps.

The most basic utility suit was the P1941 HBT pairing. This included a postwar run of jackets (produced under a 1947 contract) that bore subtle differences to the early type. It was a very simple set of jacket and trousers with open patch pockets, only three buttons up the jacket front (with a fourth to fasten the collar), and two buttons on each jacket cuff. The buttons were riveted metal "doughnut" type with "U.S. Marine Corps" around the circumference. The chest pocket included a stitched pencil pocket and the straight sleeves each had a button that could fasten into one of two buttonholes to wrap the sleeve tighter around the wrist.

The P1944 HBT jacket was a major improvement over the previous jackets, incorporating a similar single chest pocket but with a button flap and two enormous concealed pockets accessible near the center of the wearer's chest. These pockets extended from the upper chest down to the abdomen and could fit inflatable flotation bladders to aid in amphibious landings. The only indication of these concealed pockets was the stitches to the exterior of the jacket and the unusual button placement. They are later referred to as "map" or "grenade" pockets and were used however the wearer saw fit. The sleeves retained the same simple button feature.

The P1944 HBT trousers were also improved with substantial pocket space. Hip pockets similar to the Army HBT trousers closed with two buttons each and a rear pocket spanning the entire seat of the trousers, which closed using three buttons, were all of "bellows" type and were vastly superior to the simple P1941 trousers. Despite the advantage

of storage, however, many Marines unstitched the rear pocket if they preferred it.

The P1942 and P1944 reversible camouflage utility sets were also available for Marines, and though selected or issued in fewer numbers, were still worn frequently enough to be documented in many photographs. The green "jungle" side and brown "beach" side were of the same "frogskin" pattern and the P1942 jacket still included the heat-transfer Marine Corps insignia on the left breast pocket. The P1942 shared the same basic design as that of the P1941: a simple jacket with patch pockets, the one on the chest omitting the P1941's thin pencil pocket. There was only one pocket to the skirt of the jacket, positioned on the right of each side. The front closed with only three buttons or snaps and a fourth on the collar. The sleeves were straight and without the ability to be adjusted.

The P1944 camouflage jacket's improvements included button cuffs and larger, closable pockets that matched the standard P1944 HBT jacket. To simplify the reversible function, the chest pocket was omitted. The cuffs had a small open gusset that could be buttoned looser or tighter. The buttons were typically the Marine Corps "doughnut" type, though some smooth variants exist. Snaps were of a much lower profile and afforded the user the ability to wear the jacket reversibly more easily rather than having to handle buttons inside out. An additional button to the front also added more security to the closure.

The P1942 camouflage trousers had only small hip pockets and a small patch pocket per side on the rear. The hip pockets had scalloped flap closures, each with four snaps. Variations between two patterns of P1944 trousers show the first type had a series of what resembled large buttonholes around the waist, which was an experiment to simplify the reversible feature, and the second type had typical belt loops. The first type also had drawstrings around the hem called "boot blousers." Both included a series of grommets around the waist for web-belt suspenders. Some had a snap-up fly and others a button fly.

Wools

The basic wool shirt of both services prevailed, starting in the cooler months of 1951, though typically worn without the matching trousers and instead with cotton or HBT field trousers. Use of the wool shirt was not limited to cool weather, however, and the breathable shirts were used throughout the year.

The Army wool shirt first designed in 1937 as "Shirt, Flannel, Olive Drab" was gradually modified throughout World War II to include a gas flap and wrist gussets and the nomenclature appended with "Special." Both patterns were still prevalent in Korea as issue and privately purchased garments. By 1950, it retained much of its original design with the more favored "full placket" button-up front. Shoulder loops had also been adopted since the end of World War II. The new design was designated "Shirt, Flannel, Olive Drab Shade 33" and, with the trousers, the set was known generally as "OD33s." A variety of shades existed due to manufacturers' variations and an array of privately purchased and officer types that ranged from the prescribed mustard-brown color to dark-chocolate shades.

The accompanying trousers of the wool set were designed for use with the service-dress uniform and also to be worn underneath the cotton field trousers as part of the necessary layering of clothing in cold weather. Several subtle patterns existed between "Trousers, Field, Wool, Olive Drab, 22-Oz" and "Trousers, Field, Wool, Olive Drab Shade 33." They were seldom worn as an external pair of trousers

A superb image showing typical use of wool shirts with M1943 trousers and M1948 boots. The center soldier, who is possibly a KATUSA (Korean Augmentation to the United States Army), and the man to his left both wear the World War II-era M1941 shirt with simple front and no shoulder loops. Note that his gas flap is buttoned closed across his collar. The men behind him and the 60mm mortar all wear contemporary shirts with full placket and shoulder loops. Note the use of burlap helmet covers and the uncommon use of a cargo net with small-type rank insignia on the helmet of the sergeant nearest the camera. (Brennan Gauthier Collection)

An Army officer's "Shirt, Flannel, Olive Drab Shade 33" in a more "chocolate" shade and bearing the insignia of an artillery aviator. This example shows field wear and the colorful assortment of patches and badges includes a custom nametape with name, rank, and branch of service. This lieutenant flew previously for 2d Infantry Division Artillery before transferring to Korean Military Advisory Group (KMAG) for liaison-type flights. (Author's Collection)

Two Marines pose casually together in reserve. Both wear soft caps, P1941 trousers, and lace-up combat boots. The Marine on the left wears a wool shirt and based on the dark color it appears to be a P1952. His buddy wears a P1941 jacket over a five-button sweater and tucked into his trousers. (Author's Collection)

by any front-line troops and were equally uncommon among reserve units at the front.

The Marines similarly retained their wartime wool kersey or flannel shirt, which had even older roots as the P27. It was a lighter shade also referred to as "mustard" and more accurately matched that color. It was distinguishable by pointed pocket flaps that set it apart from the straight-flap Army type. The khaki shirt was of identical nomenclature and the design was also worn frequently in the field, unlike the Army, which reserved any of its khakis for use well behind the lines.

The Marine Corps design gave way to the forest-green shirt known officially as the "Shirt, USMC, P1952, Cold Weather, Wool, Flannel, Green," which matched the forest-green shade of the Marine Corps service dress. With the Marine Corps' bright-red background chevrons, the P1952 shirt made for a striking appearance and eventually supplanted the old mustard-colored shirt. Because of the use of M2-pattern buttons, it has also become known as the M2 shirt and was not incorporated into the uniform regulations until February 1961. Beyond that, there is limited documentation and it seems to be a later-war item not worn in large numbers.

Three common Army caps: from left to right, the short-brim HBT cap, the regular HBT cap, and the M1943 cap. The sagging and sloppy appearance of the HBT types is obvious compared to the nicely shaped M1943. (Author's Collection)

Two soldiers in HBT uniform wear the short-brimmed cap. The profile shot of the soldier at right shows just how small the cap could be and how little shade the brim afforded, especially when perched so far back on the head. (Author's Collection)

Caps

Both services retained their HBT soft caps from World War II. The Army issued two versions of the common HBT cap, distinguished by their short or long visor. Throughout the first year of the Korean War, it was common to see these caps worn exclusively in the field in lieu of a helmet, but this practice was stopped sometime in 1951 and the use of helmets on the static line became the norm. In an uncommon instance, personnel of at least one battalion of the 21st Infantry Regiment, the 3d Battalion, were known for wearing soft caps in lieu of helmets as a display of cockiness and *esprit de corps* (Hallahan 2003: 73).

Other visored soft caps included the "M1943 Cap, Field, Cotton, Olive Drab" and its replacement of similar style, the M1951 cap. They were both part of the winter ensemble of cotton sateen to match the M1943 system, the M1951 differing only in having a slightly longer visor and being made of the new OG-107 material. The cap contained earflaps that folded out from the interior for use in colder weather. Commanders initially liked it as an overall replacement for the HBT cap, which held little to no shape and generally exhibited a sloppy appearance. The M1943 field cap presented slightly better, but issues after laundering and discomfort during the summer months indicated another change was necessary.

Stiff blocked caps improvised from the M1943 and M1951 caps came onto the scene as a result of commanders' orders to smarten up appearance. Added plastic or cardboard helped maintain the shape of the crown and ultimately resulted in the Ridgway Cap, which dramatically changed the appearance of the common soldier. It appeared as early as 1951, but not until later in the Korean War was it widespread throughout all units; it soon became an icon of the 1950s "Atomic Era" US Army soldier. Designs were sold as a privately purchased item under names such as "Spring-up," which was the brand referenced after General Matthew B. Ridgway, commanding general of the Eighth US Army, "advocated for a better soldiering appearance." Despite the brand names, because Ridgway was responsible for the major change, the name stuck and the cap is often known as a Ridgway Cap. It was not entirely appropriate for field use, however, but well-suited for the garrison environment, units in reserve, and rear-echelon personnel.

Marines maintained their practice of wearing their cap very frequently in the field, not as an exclusive head cover, but in conjunction with the M1 helmet. Inspection of many period photographs reveals the tip of the visor peeking out below the brim of the M1 helmet. The P1944 cap was created during World War II after Marines frequently converted Army stock of the M1941 HBT cap for Marine Corps use, as the only headgear available for their tropical uniforms at the time were the garrison cap or pith helmet. The M1941 HBT cap's "conversion" was little more than the addition of an Eagle, Globe, and Anchor insignia pinned to the front and this was adopted for the P1944 cap as a permanent heat-transfer silhouette. The visor was slightly longer than the Army type and construction of the panels around the crown was dependent on application of the Marine Corps insignia. As a result, the shaping darts around the crown of the cap differ between Army and Marine Corps models to provide the latter with a solid panel of fabric across the front. The Army cap is distinguishable by the single sewn dart down the front center and a dart between the two vent eyelets on each side, while the Marine darts are repositioned to afford the flat front panel, resulting in the darts framing the vent eyelets instead. This is really the only major difference between the two caps. Unlike changes within the Army, there was no move or incentive for change away from the Marine Corps' P1944 cap and it was worn throughout the Korean War, only to be rebranded and adopted again for use with the postwar P1958 uniform set.

The pile cap became the most iconic piece of US headgear during the Korean War. The M1943 "Cap, Field, Pile, Olive Drab" had a cotton poplin exterior lined with alpaca or pile on the earflaps and visor with a wool-lined crown. It saw extremely limited use in the Mediterranean theater during World War II, but became a treasured article during the Korean winters. The cap could be worn comfortably under the helmet especially if the liner sweatband was removed.

An excellent view of the small M1948 chevrons worn on the brim of the pile cap. While many were lightly tacked on with only a few stitches or pins, this set appears well secured. Also of interest is the M1948 parka. (Author's Collection)

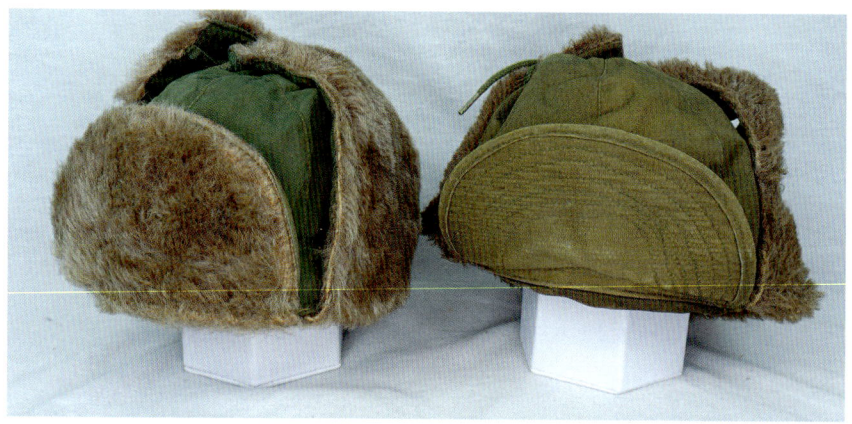

The two common variants of pile caps in Korea with and without the fur visor. Of interest is the fur-brimmed cap displayed here, which is an MQ1 type in disguise. It has a hand-applied swatch of fur to the brim and is otherwise identical to the neighboring M1951. (Author's Collection)

Two tie strings on each earflap secured the earflaps over the top of the head or under the chin and the flexible visor could be worn flipped up or down. The fur-covered visor led to general annoyance when worn down and was modified in 1948 under "Cap, Field, Pile, Olive Drab, Model Quartermaster 1 (MQ1)," which officially became "Cap, Field, Pile, M1951" in January 1951. Other manufacturers' variants exist across all variations, but the general appearance remained the same.

The pile cap became one of the most recognizable pieces of equipment of the Korean War. It was so popular during winter months that it was consistently worn under or instead of the helmet. The stiff vertical brim offered an excellent surface area for any variety of badges and insignia. Marines frequently displayed their Eagle, Globe, and Anchor badge or some type of rank insignia, especially the theater-made brass chevrons. Army soldiers similarly fixed regimental insignia or the heavy brass chevrons, but also pinned on Combat Infantryman and Medical badges, jump wings, aviator wings, cloth rank insignia, "Ranger" tabs, and more. The stand-up brim became a billboard of pride and the pile cap was arguably the most decorated piece of headwear among both services for officers and enlisted men alike.

An interior view of the pile cap variants showing slight difference in nomenclature. Both show the alpaca lining and instructions for wear with earflaps up, down, and under helmet. (Author's Collection)

From left to right: the Marine Corps M1951 boot, the M1948 boot, and the M1943 double-buckle boot. All show signs of heavy use, particularly the Army boots, which have nearly smooth soles from wear. Note the dull "rough out" texture of the Marine Corps boots and the double buckles (which have been polished enough to smooth down the texture) in contrast to the shiny M1948 boots. (Author's Collection)

Footwear

The "double-buckle" or "two-buckle" boot produced during World War II was initially the predominant combat boot worn by US forces in Korea. The M1943 "Boot, Service, Combat" was the standard Army issue and used frequently within the Marine Corps as well. The main boot was constructed of reversed leather that originally required dubbing to be waterproof, though this was not enforced in Korea. Troops still practiced similar waterproofing methods, however, resulting in smooth, nearly polished leather to match the buckle-cuff upper.

Soldiers eventually began to adopt the M1948 boot known as "Boot, Service, Combat, Russet." Styled after the World War II paratrooper boot, it was a lace-up, cap-toe boot that provided excellent support and could be polished well for garrison duty with effort. The exterior required some scraping, smoothing, burn-polishing, and spit-shining to become smooth, shiny, and reflective. The M1948 boot was not initially an issue item nor was it ever available in large quantities, but it was very popular and soldiers found ways to acquire or purchase them. It was presentable, solved problems of the M1943 boot- cuff and buckles

BELOW LEFT
This image shows the color and texture of buckle boots. The lowers are soft suede and the uppers stiffer and more easily polished. Note the sweater worn under HBTs and the chinstrap clasped around the back brim of the helmet. (Author's Collection)

BELOW RIGHT
A soldier in reserve enjoying his pipe exhibits fairly well polished and clean M1948 boots. His trousers are very tightly cinched around the cuff of the boot, likely with the help of something like a blousing band. His cap appears new and not yet broken in. (Author's Collection)

A chow line shows a full array of soldiers wearing Mickey Mouse boots. This photograph captures an instance of uniformity in which all the men appear to wear the same uniform, including the M1948 parka, and have their field gear arranged in the same way. Their helmets appear smooth and fairly glossy and bear the insignia of the 5th Regimental Combat Team. (Brennan Gauthier Collection)

A Korean Service Corps worker carries new winter boots to a front-line Marine Corps company, November 1951. (DoD photo #A158079)

snagging on vegetation and debris, and offered the desired look of the paratrooper-style boot.

The Marine Corps started with the basic N-1 service shoe, known as the "boondocker," which was worn with lace-up leggings. The Marine Corps also transitioned to a lace-up boot of their own pattern. The M1951 combat boot featured hooks on the upper cuff for speed lacing and a reinforced backstay. As was typical, the Marine Corps was slower to catch up to the Army and maintained use of boondockers with leggings until later in the Korean War. During the defense of the Pusan Perimeter in 1950, the North Koreans used the nickname "Yellow Leg Devils" for the Marines in reference to their khaki leggings.

Shoepacs were the most common boot issued for cold and cold–wet weather in the Korean theater during the 1950/51 cold season. A now-classic style of winter boot, the shoepac design is similar to the recognizable winter boot made popular by Leon L. Bean in 1911, with a waterproof rubber sole and leather upper. The "Shoepac, 12-inch, M1944" issued to both Army and Marine Corps troops in Korea had a black rubber lower and sole and dark-brown oiled leather upper with rawhide laces. The shoepac was most appropriate for the soggy fall and spring. In colder temperatures, however, the boots trapped moisture after marching or other activity, resulting in more cases of frostbite due to the moisture freezing inside the boot. Instructions were to change socks frequently and dry damp pairs against the chest, but the intensity of the winter fighting made such a task prohibitive. As a result, many troops discarded their shoepacs or avoided them in favor of the basic combat boot.

During the winter of 1951/52, the insulated rubber combat boot became available. Known as the "Mickey Mouse Boot" due to its large size and black color, it was considered superior to the shoepac. Designed to be effective to -20 degrees Fahrenheit, it was constructed of two layers of rubber with wool insulation in between to retain heat within the boot and block out cold air and moisture. Despite the improvements and effort to reduce the shortcomings of the shoepac, particularly the incessant sock changing, the Mickey Mouse boot became just as notorious for trapping moisture under combat circumstances. Regardless, it was a welcome improvement in the harshest winter conditions.

COLD-WEATHER ATTIRE

M1943 and M1951 field uniforms

The M1943 field jacket variants were by far the most popular outer garments among both Army and Marine Corps personnel during the colder months following the winter of 1950/51. After World War II, plans to introduce a button-in liner (to replace or supplement the M1943 pile liner) prompted modifications to existing M1943 field jackets, which were rebranded "MQ-1" during first production in 1948 and later produced under the nomenclature "M1950." These were identical in style except for internal buttons to accept the liner. The only other major change was in sizing, the traditional numbered sizes being updated with a simplified range of letter sizes. Substantial numbers of World War II-produced field jackets were modified with the additional buttons and updated size tags. Those that remained in the supply system were supplemented by Eighth US Army with an issue of ten plastic buttons that were to be sewn inside by the wearer. As a result, the issued field jackets in Korea included all variants of the M1943, MQ-1, and M1950.

Even when worn without either liner, the field jacket served as an excellent windbreaker against the icy Manchurian gusts. The matching button-in liner went into production in December 1950, but was not issued until spring 1951. The M1943 pile liner remained dominant as an intermediate layer. During rainy seasons, the hood was often buttoned onto the collar.

The accompanying M1943 trousers that completed the "suit" could be chosen for wear in climates that required the field jacket. This resulted in a mixture of troops wearing HBT trousers (offering generous pocket

Soldiers wearing the classic M1943 field uniform; only the soldier sitting at left appears to wear HBTs instead. Both soldiers in the foreground wear the 7th Infantry Division unit patch, though on the corporal in center it is barely visible. He also wears the M1948 chevrons. The men flanking him have private chevrons on their helmets. Note the M1945 suspenders clasped together across the chest; it appears to be a consistent practice for all soldiers in this photograph. (Author's Collection)

The M1943 field jacket shown here is representative of a garrison type worn by many Army officers in Korea. It includes only the necessary insignia of cloth rank and the 2d Infantry Division unit patch. This example was worn prior to September 19, 1951, when its owner, Lieutenant Peter H. Monfore, was killed at Heartbreak Ridge. (Author's Collection)

This lieutenant of the 32d Infantry Regiment (7th Infantry Division) wears a brand-new M1951 field jacket and matching trousers on Thanksgiving Day 1952. The zipper and snap(s) can be seen in the open collar and he uses the leg ties as intended. Of interest are his leather pocket hanger name tag, rank insignia on shoulders and pile cap visor, and a private-purchase revolver in custom holster. (Author's Collection)

space) or the simpler but warmer and durable M1943 trousers. They were produced in olive-drab cotton sateen to match the jacket and few variations exist outside of manufacturers' differences. The only major variations concern "rigger"-modified trousers that were common only within airborne and other special units. The addition of large pockets on the thighs originated during World War II to match the previously issued M1942 jump suit. The pleated pockets closed with a snap flap and had long ties to wrap around the leg and secure the pockets' contents for airborne operations.

An updated version of the uniform came in the form of the M1951 model. A fair number of photographs from as early as 1952 reveal use of the M1951 trousers, but the M1951 field jackets came much later, in 1953. The trousers were made of the same cotton sateen as the previous model, but with large cargo pockets in addition to the hip and rear pockets.

The M1941 field jacket

While the M1943 field jacket prevailed and parkas remained popular, the early World War II-type M1941 field jacket also found its way into the supply system. The thin cotton poplin "khaki" (OD No. 3) jacket with a wool liner was of waist length with slash pockets on the abdomen. It was intended as an outer garment to be worn in cool and cold conditions and was an iconic jacket for the World War II soldier until the M1943 overtook it as a replacement. General daily wear and especially combat use battered the jacket and it suffered frayed cuffs and collars. Despite its age and subject to wear, it was surprisingly popular in the Korean theater, not only in rear-echelon units but with front-line troops as well.

Tailored jackets

In-theater tailored jackets also began to appear. The majority were styled after the World War II winter combat "tanker jacket" made exclusively for armored personnel. The popular design had a short waist, and elastic cuffs, collar, and waistband, and both civilian and theater-made models were worn in Korea. A vast array of variants appeared in many materials ranging from cotton poplin to durable twill, lighter shades of khaki to dark greens and olive drab, silk or rayon-quilted linings or wool, and a range of styles and cuts of elastic cuffs, collars, and waistbands. The overall appearance remained consistent, with the only major variations outside of material and construction being additional chest or sleeve pockets.

The soldier standing wears the M1941 jacket. The author estimates this photograph to date from February 1952. The cap in his right hand appears stiff as if it is a Ridgway cap or M1943 cap reinforced with a stiffener. His left sleeve shows the wearing of insignia and though unclear, it is known to be that of the 7th Infantry Division. (Author's Collection)

Reflective of the styling of the M1941 field jacket, this theater-made garment with 45th Infantry Division insignia has a thin cotton shell with a wool lining made from material from a sleeping bag or wool blanket. It shows significant field use with evident tattering and staining. Loose stitching on the sergeant first class chevrons reveals darker, unfaded areas beneath which the smaller M1948-type chevrons in lower grade of sergeant were once affixed. (Author's Collection)

The M1943 pile liner

Among the most popular garments for the frigid Korean winters was the M1943 pile liner. Though the manufacturer's tag explicitly states "not to be worn as an outer garment," its use as such was prevalent in the Army and Marines throughout the Korean War. It became common practice to wear it as a result of its simplicity, comfort, and supply shortages of outer field jackets. During the winter of 1950/51 it was typically worn as suggested as an undergarment beneath whichever parka or jacket was worn as the outermost garment. The majority of M1943 pile liners, particularly World War II-dated production, had alpaca lining, but some manufacturers' variations do exist sporting HBT or rayon interiors due to emergency production for use in Korea in 1950. These variants arrived at the front in 1951. The liner was extremely warm and insulating especially once the wearer was moving around marching, digging, or fighting.

The winter Marine

Where the Army was initially short on cold-weather gear, the Marine Corps issued equipment more effectively beginning in October 1950. The Marine Corps heavy lined parka with hood was worn over the field

A soldier posing with a Thompson submachine gun wears the pile liner as an exterior garment. The rest of his uniform consists of M1943 trousers, shoepacs, and a pile cap of unclear style. (Author's Collection)

This pile liner, unlike most of the items in the author's collection, was unissued and shows a strong green OD No. 7 color that retains much of the sheen of new sateen cotton. As a standalone item, it could present a somewhat unstylish appearance, but was extremely practical and favored as a garment in the field. (Author's Collection)

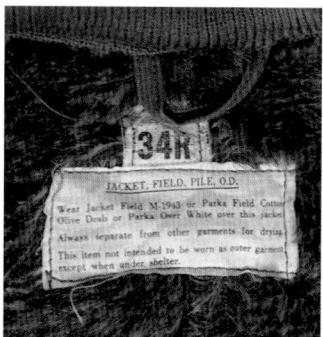

jacket and extended down to about 12in above the boot. Some of those issued came from stocks of the 1947 Navy Deck Parka. Both Marine and Navy types had very similar construction to the Army parka-type overcoat, but the Marine Corps pattern was nearly indistinguishable from its cousin at a distance. The major differences upon close inspection were a light-duty brass zipper, darker "chocolate" color alpaca lining, and button tabs at the waist rather than an integral belt. The Navy parkas had a single breast pocket with "U.S.N." stamp, cloth belt with slide buckle, and two lower pockets on the skirt with angled flaps.

The Marines utilized lined trigger-finger mittens or leather work gloves with liners, pile caps, shoepacs, and layer upon layer of fatigues, wools, underwear, sweaters, and vests to keep warm. In many instances, equipment such as gloves and winter boots was simply not available and so Marines fought wearing whatever they had. One Marine (George McMaster) explicitly recalled his entire uniform for the Chosin campaign as follows: one green T-shirt (or skivvy shirt) and one green pair of shorts, put on in the morning of October 26; one pair of long johns and one sweatshirt, received at Hamhung; one long-sleeved khaki flannel shirt; one short-sleeved wool sweater; one dungaree jacket; one field jacket; one fur-lined parka; two pairs of dungaree pants; two pairs of socks; one pair of summer field shoes; and one pair of canvas leggings.

A popular item among Marines was the alpaca-lined vest. Initially manufactured in 1942 and first used in North China during the occupation of 1945–48, it was intended for cold-weather duty that required moderate to heavy physical activity for which bulkier equipment would inhibit movement. The vest was to be worn under the field jacket or parka, or alone as an outer garment in milder weather. It had a durable cotton poplin exterior with alpaca lining to match that of the parka and pile jacket. The front bore no pockets and later versions manufactured during the Korean War incorporated splits at the bottom of the side

Marines at the Chosin Reservoir in November 1950 wear fairly adequate winter attire of parkas, shoepacs, and mittens. Those clear to the camera have their socks pulled high above the cuff of the boot with their trousers tucked into the socks. This perspective from behind shows the tremendous load on their backs, including sleeping bags, blankets, and shelter-halves or ponchos in addition to their basic equipment. (US Department of Defense Marine Corps Photo)

A clear full view of the M1948 parka, showing the fur hood, sleeve pocket, and exposed drawstring across the waist. (Author's Collection)

seams. It was almost exclusively a Marine Corps-issued piece of clothing, though some use by Army personnel has been observed and such examples can only be inferred to have been traded or looted.

Army parkas and field overcoats

Several types of parkas and overcoats were issued by the Army and were the most appropriate choice for winter temperatures, despite their fit, which often prohibited more comfortable movement in combat conditions. The "Overcoat, Parka Type, with Pile Liner" appears to have been one of the most commonly issued during the winter of 1950/51, particularly to artillerymen, engineers, and other supporting arms. It was a skirted, fur-lined garment with a belt threaded through sewn loops. The belt was the same model as the enlisted man's belt with an open buckle of blackened metal. A set of covered slash pockets were above the belt and below were two very large patch pockets on the skirt with an exposed button flap. The liner was removable, but not typically worn separately. Adjustable cuffs concealed elastic cuffs and the zipper was of heavy-duty zinc. The fur lining can be seen in different variations of the alpaca type used on the M1943 pile liner and also a creamy white.

The other styles of parka most frequently used during the first winter in Korea were the surplus designs developed for ski troops of the 10th Mountain Division during World War II. The two anorak-style "Parka, Field, Cotton" and the "Parka, Ski, Reversible" were widely used; they offered little insulation, but were excellent windbreakers. When the 7th Infantry Division landed at Iwon in October 1950, its personnel were almost entirely equipped with the reversible parka as an outer garment. It could be worn with a wolf-fur trim around the hood, but this seems to have been largely omitted by the time of the Korean War. Both designs shared a similar baggy appearance, with a hem below the waist, a hood, three-button collar, and two slash pockets on the chest that provided access to a large center pocket. To mitigate the inadequacy of insulation, soldiers wore the pile liner, wools or HBTs (or both), and winter underwear underneath.

The third mountain-troop garment issued from Army stock was the reversible "parka-type" overcoat. A predecessor to the parka-type overcoat, this garment was a lighter, greener olive-drab color and included a thin canvas belt that threaded through sewn loops. The clasp was identical to the M1 helmet chinstrap material and fastener. Above the belt were two open slash pockets and below were two smaller patch

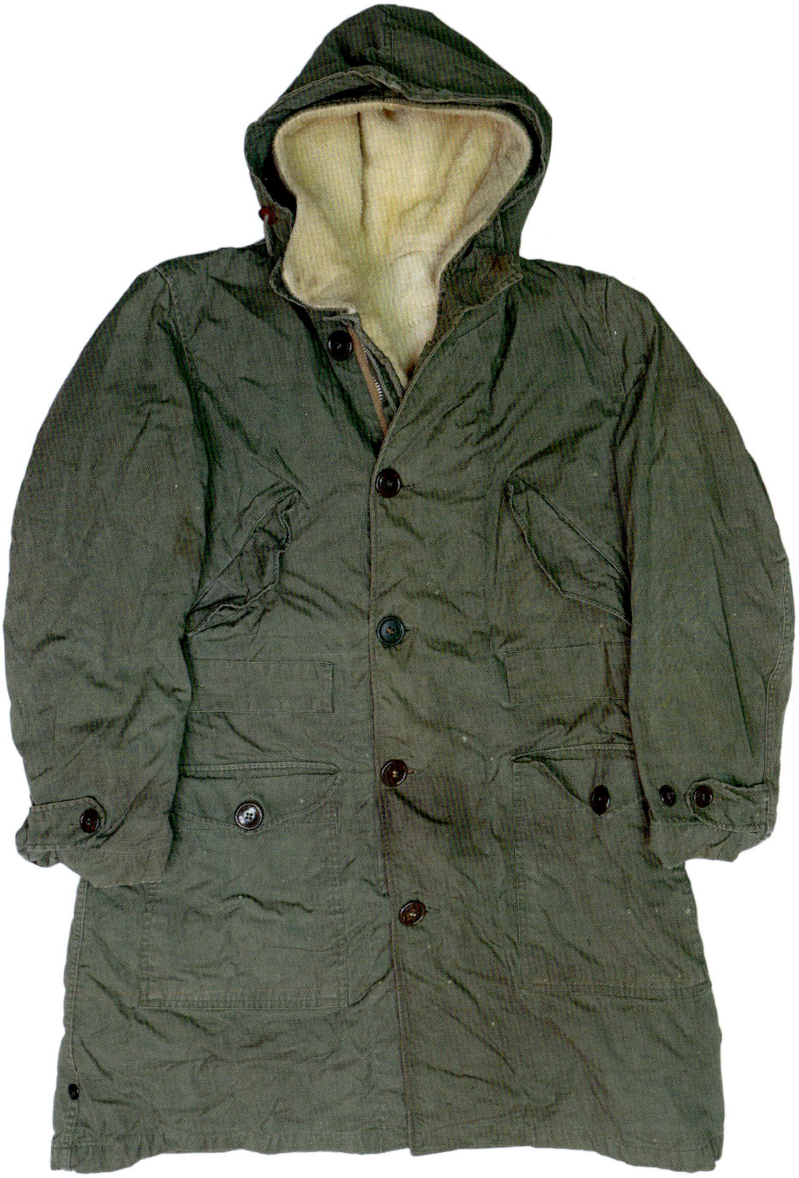

This example of the "Overcoat, Parka Type, with Pile Liner" lacks the cloth belt with buckle and has several flaws indicating quick field repairs. Despite being issued to an Army officer, the label reveals it is US Air Force issue and may be related to the variation in off-white lining rather than typical olive drab. The author finds this to be of interest as it represents how the different parts of the US armed forces called on each other to address supply shortages during the brutal winters in Korea. (Author's Collection)

A lieutenant of the 32d Infantry Regiment (7th Infantry Division), looking miserable in the Korean winter, wears the cold-weather attire of late 1952. His M1948 parka can be identified by the left sleeve pocket. He wears trigger-finger mittens, insulated rubber "Mickey Mouse" boots, and an M1951 pile cap with rank insignia. His lack of web equipment indicates that he is likely in reserve or otherwise "off line." (Author's Collection)

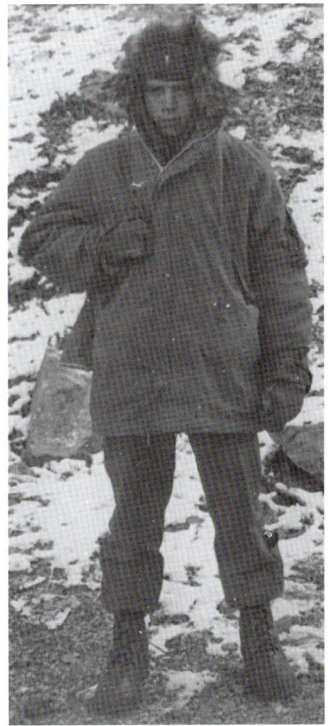

pockets. The white side had no pockets, but both sides featured a zipper front concealed with buttons. Frequently worn "green" side out, the reversible type is distinguishable in photographs because of the large flash of white exposed by the open hood and collar.

The M1948 parka, a simple zip-up design with snap closure and two large angled pockets on the lower chest, also included a hooded, snap-in, wool pile liner. Intended to replace the parka-type overcoat, it was adopted in 1949 and approved in late July 1950, but only produced for one year after it was found to be expensive and somewhat complicated to manufacture. It received its nickname, "fishtail" parka, because of the split on the back hem. A concealed drawstring offered waist adjustment while another drawstring along the bottom hem allowed for pulling tight against the legs. The integral hood was framed with a significant amount of wolf fur. On the left sleeve was an additional cigarette-type pocket.

A cheery soldier posing in February 1952 while in reserve. He wears a soft cap, HBT trousers, and the high-neck sweater worn by both Army and Marine personnel. Issued throughout the cold months, the World War II-era "Sweater, High Neck" was a pullover wool garment with a tall collar closed by five buttons, earning its alternate name as the "five-button sweater." (Author's Collection)

A useful close-up image displaying leather gloves with wool inserts. Both the brown World War II-pattern glove and black M1949 glove were made from horsehide leather, a very durable material; they were favored as a working glove, often worn by artillerymen handling ammunition, and used in winter out of necessity. Three varieties of trigger-finger mitten also existed: "Mitten-Shells, Trigger Finger," and two later variants noted by the suffix "Type 1" and later "M1948." All three came with wool inserts. The shell was a cotton outer that extended above the wrist in a gauntlet style with a web strap slide-buckle adjustment on the wrist. The palm was a tan shade of leather deerskin. (Author's Collection)

The M1951 parka eventually came to replace the other parkas used by US troops. Production began one year after the approval of the previous M1948 parka, but the new model did not make it to Korea until much later in the war. The M1951 had a simple liner without hood; the hood of the outer shell could receive a fur-trimmed hood, which was produced as a separate item. The sleeve pocket was omitted, but the fit and style of the M1951 was largely identical to the M1948. It was one of the first items made with the new OG-107 color instead of the classic olive drab. The liner was made of mohair frieze instead of wool pile. While it was scheduled to be issued to a majority of troops, by 1953 there was still only limited supply amounting to less than one-quarter of the quantity required for winter distribution.

Overwhite parkas were issued in limited quantities and only used when snow covered the ground. Anecdotal reference to these from the 179th Infantry Regiment detailed a snow suit of "silk like" items consisting of trousers with drawstring, hooded pullover, and gloves. These were only issued for patrols when there was sufficient snow on the ground. The hood had a drawstring that was cinched tightly around the face to reveal the wearer's eyes only. Field gear and bandoleers were worn over the snow suit, which was consistently noted throughout its use during the Korean War to be a problem, as the dark olive-drab webbing contrasted starkly with the white camouflage. Soldiers additionally wrapped their rifles with white medical tape for these patrols. The reference to "silk like" is unclear, as the typical overwhite parka was manufactured of oxford cloth.

A popular outer garment for cold weather was the field overcoat. Among the variations, the most widely issued was the "Overcoat, Field, Olive Drab 7, with Removable Liner," later amended with the suffix "M1950." It was a trench coat-style, double-breasted design including a cloth belt with slide buckle, wide lapels, button cuffs, and slash pockets on the front. It extended below the knee and included a button-in wool liner. Adequate quantities were issued to supporting arms and many officers of all branches frequently donned the garment.

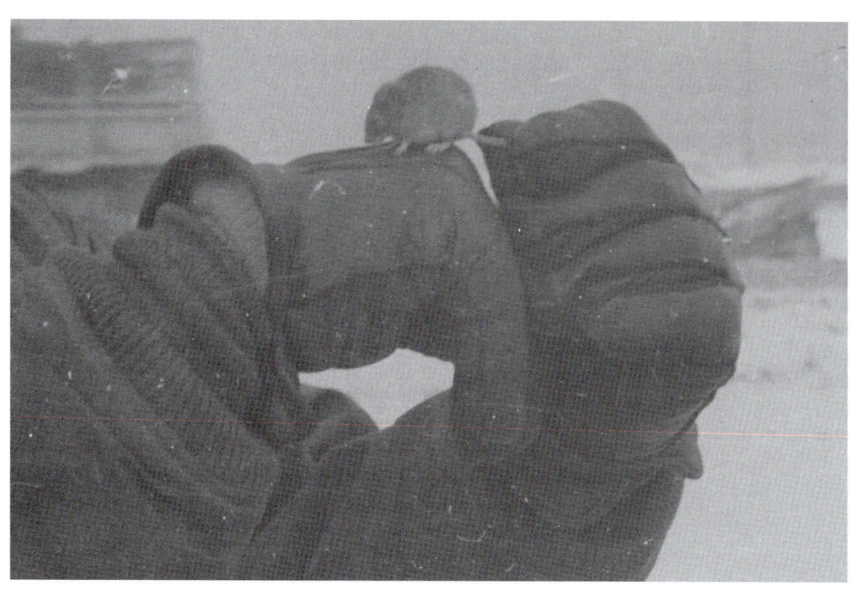

FIELD GEAR AND EQUIPMENT

Helmets

Most helmets used in Korea were produced during World War II with a front seam or rear seam, stainless or manganese rim, predominantly with swivel loops for the chinstraps. These were both OD No. 3 and OD No. 7 sewn on with a range of hardware materials depending on production years. The shells ranged from new stock to showing some abuse and several layers of repaint. The helmet liners received overhauls in 1951 until the end of the Korean War, when many were re-webbed with OD No. 7 material and relabeled with the latest date by companies such as CAPAC and Micarta.

The Marines arrived in Korea in August 1950 without their camouflage helmet covers, but all units after the 1st Provisional Marine Brigade had the iconic cover. Conversely, the Army had yet to adopt any kind of official helmet cover. Around mid-1952, the use of sandbags for helmet covers became widely practiced. These are not to be confused with the short-lived green helmet covers officially produced and issued, though no quantities of these made it to Korea in any known capacity until after the armistice. The author knows of only one documented helmet cover issued to a Turkish officer in 1954.

Army use of helmet nets was rare in Korea. Those worn ranged in type from the ¼in-mesh Type 1 (which came with an elastic camouflage band), the common ¾in British Mk 2 (adopted as the Type 2), and the large 2in type cut from vehicle netting. The elastic camouflage band was used fairly frequently on its own in the early days of the Korean War.

Two artillery officers observing from a hilltop show their embellished helmets. The officer to the left is likely Division Artillery as he has the 24th Infantry Division insignia on the left side of his helmet. The officer crouching and pointing is Lieutenant Colonel Jack J. Kron, commander of the 52d Field Artillery Battalion, with that unit's insignia displayed on the left side of his helmet. Both show metal rank soldered to the front of their helmets. The right side of Kron's helmet is known to have had the 24th Infantry Division insignia. (Author's Collection)

A group of Marines wearing three different varieties of helmets and helmet covers. On the left is the mosquito-net cover, identifiable by the integrated elastic band. The other Marines show a mix of bare helmets and Marine Corps-pattern helmet covers, which appear to be "beach" side out. Note the P1941 suspenders on the Marine at far left, cross-flap canteens, shovels, and the poncho slung over the cartridge belt worn by the Marine to the right. (US Navy Medicine Photo #09-7952-11)

23

Members of the 3d Airborne Ranger Company prepare for a mission and exhibit a variety of equipment. At left is an automatic rifleman with the M1937 BAR belt. The soldier at center, obscured by the sergeant, also wears this belt as does the Ranger at right and slightly out of focus. Most wear lace-up combat boots, which are likely to be paratrooper boots, while two or three wear buckle boots. Ponchos are folded over belts or rolled up and secured on suspenders, and many wear soft caps under their helmets. The sergeant first class third from right wears small M1948 chevrons below 3d Infantry Division insignia below "Ranger" and "Airborne" tabs. (US Signal Corps Photo #SC-365634)

Web gear

Soldiers and Marines of the Korean War used the same basic loadout as their World War II counterparts. The Army had largely transitioned from light-khaki (OD No. 3) web equipment to the olive-drab (OD No. 7) shade, but the Marines still had a large quantity of early World War II "782" gear to use.

The M1945 pack system had become the standard for both officers and men of the Army. The pack was a modular design based on the Marine Corps system with an upper "Pack, Field, Combat" and lower "Pack, Field, Cargo" that relied on the matching "Suspenders, Pack, Field" for carriage. The packs were constructed of OD No. 7 cotton canvas, and had rubberized linings and a series of exterior straps to connect. The upper combat pack included interior divisions to organize mess-kit components, rations, and essential items such as socks and underwear. On the exterior were straps to secure the shelter-half over

This view of a typical Army rifleman cartridge-belt assembly shows the most basic amenities worn without a pack or suspenders. Attached to the M1923 cartridge belt are the scabbard for an M1942 bayonet, the covers for an M1943 entrenching tool and an M1910 canteen, and an M1942 first-aid kit; a Mk 2 fragmentation grenade is also shown. (Author's Collection)

(continued on page 33)

THE WAR BEGINS, SUMMER 1950
1: Private, 24th Infantry Division, summer 1950
2: Staff Sergeant, 1st Provisional Marine Brigade, August 1950
3: Private, 1st Marine Division, September 1950

A

MOBILE WARFARE, LATE 1950
1: Corporal, 1st Cavalry Division, October 1950
2: Lieutenant Colonel, 7th Infantry Division, November 1950
3: Private, 1st Marine Division, December 1950

B

SPRING 1951
1: Private, 187th Airborne Regimental Combat Team
(Airborne), May 1951
2: Corporal, 3d Airborne Ranger Company, 3d Infantry
Division, April 1951
3: Sergeant, 2d Infantry Division, spring 1951

1951–52

1: Lieutenant, artillery,
25th Infantry Division,
autumn 1951

2: Private first class, field
artillery, summer 1951

3: Private, 40th Infantry
Division, February 1952

D

**BODY ARMOR AND
BEHIND THE LINES, 1952**
1: Sergeant, 1st Marine
Division, spring 1952
2: Soldier, infantry,
summer 1952
3: Private first class, 17th
Infantry Regiment, 7th
Infantry Division, 1952

POSITIONAL WARFARE, 1952 -53
1: Private, a replacement company, winter 1952
2: Sergeant, 5th Regimental Combat Team, 1953
3: Brigadier general, IX Corps, 1952

F

IN THE FIELD, 1952 -53
1: First sergeant, 45th Infantry
Division, 1953
2: Sergeant first class, engineer
combat battalion, 1952
3: Private first class, medical
company, 1952

G

SPECIALISTS, 1953

1: Captain, aviation detachment, 1953
2: Sergeant, tank battalion, 1953
3: Private, military police, Eighth US Army, 1953

H

the top, a center tab with grommets to hold the entrenching tool, and a similar tab on the wearer's left for the bayonet. The lower pack, which held spare clothing and other nonessentials, could be dropped as required by quick-release straps. It also included a handle so it could be used as a furlough bag. The upper combat pack similarly could easily be detached from the suspenders by simple buckles near the shoulder. The set was worn mostly when marching or, as the Korean War progressed, dropped completely as movement became limited to short patrols. Riflemen were more likely to retain the suspenders after the pack was removed to support the weight of 80 rounds of .30-06 ammunition.

Regulations specified the arrangement of equipment on the individual soldier to be precise and non-variable. For officers and noncommissioned officers, moving clockwise on the M1936 pistol belt from the right hip: the first-aid pouch, pistol, entrenching tool (if carried), canteen above the left buttock, bayonet on the left hip, and pistol-ammunition pouch at left front. Despite this order, photographs show all possible arrangements depending on the wearer's preference and substitution or addition of the carbine-ammunition pouch if it was carried.

There was little variation in the style of the basic equipment issued. Riflemen wore the basic M1923 ten-pocket cartridge belt with 10in M1942 bayonet. Automatic riflemen and their assistants both wore the appropriate M1937 BAR cartridge belt. The first-aid pouch was the M1942 Carlisle pouch with waxed cardboard insert and the canteen carrier was the M1910, all predominantly OD No. 7 for the Army but a large quantity of khaki and OD No. 3 for the Marine Corps.

Those troops armed with carbines – either the semiautomatic M1 or the select-fire M2 – wore the pistol belt, typically with one or more ammunition pouches for the 15-round magazines. The buttstock-style pouch "Pocket, Magazine, Double Web, Carbine M1" was also frequently used appropriately on the carbine stock. This original design had an open sleeve back with snap to secure it on the pistol belt. The updated model dropped the snap and simplified the reverse with two short web straps, limiting its use to wearing on the belt. It was rebranded as "Pocket, Cart., Cal 30 M1, Carbine or Rifle" and included two grommets to hang other gear of the M1910 system. Later in the Korean War as flak vests hindered comfortable wear of the cartridge belt and bulk ammunition was available in bunkers, it became quite common for soldiers to use the carbine pouch to store only a couple of en bloc clips for the M1 Garand.

The new box pouch that could hold up to five magazines was not readily available either. Typically, two of the high-capacity magazines were issued with the M2 carbine. The magazines were frequently taped together and simply left in the weapon and loaded through the breech using ten-round stripper clips.

Carbines were issued with the M4 bayonet, frequently carried as a knife for those who did not wield a carbine. Though wear on the hip was typical, many troops armed with a pistol carried the blade behind their holster, but there are many instances of soldiers and Marines carrying the bayonet on the ankle.

A very rare photograph depicting an Army medic. His visible equipment is the large medical kit bag slung across his body to rest on his right hip and what appears to be a general-purpose bag slung opposite. The "Medical Kit, Individual" had replaced the harness system used by Army medics in World War II and was greatly simplified in that the large bag was slung by a single strap. Aside from this item, medical personnel were not identified by any armbands or markings that would make them a target. The first medics in Korea were specifically targeted and rapidly adapted to the very hostile enemy. In addition to ditching their red-cross brassards and helmet insignia, they also began to arm themselves. From the few images available of Navy Corpsmen attached to Marine Corps units, it appears that they incorporated the same large bag into their kit, replacing previous systems used during World War II. (Author's Collection)

A paratrooper preparing for a training jump is loaded with a parachute on his back, reserve parachute near his abdomen, and an upper pack with shelter-half below that. The dangling chinstrap on his helmet exhibits the webbed chincup exclusive to the M1-C helmet and liner. He wears T-7 parachute system with his carbine slung vertically through the harness. His hands rest on the reserve chute on his front. Below that is a M1945 pack with shelter-half strapped horseshoe style. It is unclear how his canteen is secured as no pistol belt is visible. Note the small-type private first class chevron on his sleeve below 187th Regimental Combat Team (Airborne) insignia. (Author's Collection)

Grenades were typically carried hooked over the belt or in the large uniform pockets, but occasionally a soldier can be seen wearing the two- or three-pocket grenade pouch. Rifle-ammunition bandoleers were popular at the start of the Korean War and riflemen often marched and fought with as many as four draped across the body. The emerging static warfare by 1951 changed this practice and replenishment of ammunition came courtesy of Korean porters lugging large quantities in metal ammunition boxes.

Entrenching tools were carried on packs or belts as needed. Once the war stabilized into fixed positions, however, entrenching tools tended to be left in bunkers with other items of personal gear not needed throughout each day. Both the Army and Marines used the M1943 folding shovel as the basic entrenching tool. A modification to this in September 1945 included an added pick on the opposite side to the spade. These early models were retrofitted M1943 shovels; later, the M1951 tool was introduced as a newly produced model that included the pick feature.

Other personal entrenching tools included the M1910 Pick Mattock and the M1910 axe. The author does not recall seeing either tool carried by individual soldiers or Marines in photographs; it is likely that these tools were less popular during the Korean War as such equipment was available on vehicles and later in bunkers.

All manner of specialized equipment was issued and used appropriately: binoculars in a leather carrying case for officers and observer types; compasses with a chemically impregnated compass pouch; radios; and packboards for large loads. Other specialized equipment for ammunition included the M2A1 carrying vest and the M1 and M6 bags for bazooka, recoilless-rifle, and mortar rounds. A stacked three-pocket carrying case was also popular for carrying grenades or any other item an individual deemed necessary. The general-purpose "Bag, Carrying, Ammunition" was still in circulation and the new "Case, Magazine, 30 Round, Submachine Gun" was issued for use with M3 or Thompson submachine guns.

Ponchos were essential during the rainy seasons and often folded neatly over the back center of the belt. The Army poncho was a simple olive-drab pullover large enough to go over a soldier's entire set of field gear and close tight around the collar by means of a drawstring. It was a World War II design updated in 1949 and constructed of nylon twill coated in vinyl resin to repel water effectively. An update in 1951 added a hood. Unchanged from World War II, the Marine Corps poncho was reversible with green and brown sides to match their typical reversible patterns. It was hoodless and closed by a choice of three snaps on the collar.

In addition to a being personal garment, the poncho was used in place of shelter-halves (if none of the latter were available) as a rudimentary waterproof cover, a blackout curtain for viewing maps by light at night, or a protective layer against damp or saturated ground. Ponchos were also a common cover for the bodies of those killed in action.

Only for Marines

The P1941 pack system was a World War II design that was extremely functional though somewhat complicated due to the number of straps necessary to secure the upper (haversack) and lower (knapsack) packs to the suspenders as well as affordances for bedrolls, shelter-halves, or ponchos. The camouflage shelter-half was typically wrapped over the top of the upper pack in horseshoe style. An ordinary Marine's full complement of equipment in addition to the pack system included his cartridge belt or pistol belt with canteens, bayonet, and first-aid kit(s).

The jungle first-aid kit was somewhat exclusive to the Marines in Korea. First appearing in August 1943 and subject to some modifications through World War II, it had three compartments for a greater variety of medical supplies than the standard small Carlisle pouch. A series of flaps closed over the contents, with the main one bearing two standard snaps rather than lift-the-dot fastening. It contained solution for athlete's foot, iodine, insect repellent, sulfadiazine, water-purification tablets, a vial of atabrine tablets, bandages, and field dressings. This first-aid kit had significantly more components than the Army's M1942 Carlisle bandage kit, which was limited and basically intended for one-time use.

The practice of carrying two canteens carried through to Korea and the Marines' cross-flap or "dog-ear" canteen cover was issued from World War II stock. It was another piece of the Marine Corps' field equipment that was absolutely iconic, exclusive to the Corps, and could identify a Marine instantly from a distance. The final design of the unlined canvas

This pistol belt holds what a Marine officer or NCO might carry while wielding a carbine. The assembly along the M1942 pistol belt includes a World War I vintage pistol-magazine pouch, M4 bayonet in M8 sheath, two canteens (one Marine "dog-ear" P3 type and one Army M1942 type), folded M1942 poncho, M1916 pistol holster, and M1942 first-aid pouch. There is little room to spare for anything else. All carbine ammunition is carried as stripper clips in the bandoleer. (Author's Collection)

Two Marines investigating a North Korean dugout during operations around Seoul clearly display some of their equipment. The Marine at right appears to be an assistant gunner as he wears an M1937 BAR belt but carries an M1 Garand rifle with a regular bandoleer. His suspenders are either M1936 or M1945 type and he carries two Army-type canteens. The Marine at left has the P1941 upper combat pack and suspenders with entrenching tool on the back and a rocket tube across the top secured by the upper strap. From his cartridge belt hang a P1941 canteen, jungle first-aid kit, and something like a poncho folded over the back of the belt. Both Marines wear P1944 trousers. (US Department of Defense Marine Corps Photo #A-2819)

cover included a stitched hole on the bottom to aid in efficiently filling canteens from trailers or jerry cans. Both earlier Marine covers like the P1941 similarly styled Army M1910 insulated covers were also issued to Marines and all types can be seen worn alongside one another. Ultimately, the M1910 cover became the standard design as the cross-flap cover was phased out, but the Corps held on to it through the Korean War.

The Marines seemed to retain their exclusive combination pistol and carbine ammunition pouch which, like the 1911 pistol-magazine pouches, stood in contrast to OD No. 3 and OD No. 7 gear as it was a more mustardy shade of khaki.

Navy corpsmen tending to a wounded Marine show at left the large medical kit bag also used by the Army. The corpsman in the center bending over shows a cross-flap canteen, jungle first-aid kit, and Army-type canteen as well as an M4 bayonet and pistol. Most wear P1944 trousers except the corpsman at left who wears P1941 trousers. An interesting mix of gear is worn including wool shirts, Army HBT jacket, and a sweater worn by the man obscured in shadow in the center. (US Navy Medicine Photo #09-7952-9)

Flak vests

The Korean War was the major testing ground for individual body armor. Beginning in June 1951, a joint Army/Navy mission began field-testing prototypes and by early 1952, the flak vest was recognized as a necessity and became available in quantity. Initially, the Marine Corps supplied both themselves and the Army with their M1951 vest while the Army continued to test its own versions. Until they settled on a final design, Army soldiers used World War II-issue Army Air Corps M1 body armor (in very limited numbers), M12 armor vests, and prototype T1952 variants.

As early as November 1951, the Marine Corps had standardized its design for a flak vest, which used a combination of overlapping doron plates across the flatter areas of the vest and 12-ply basket-weave nylon for flexible areas. By July 1952, all or most front-line Marine Corps personnel had been equipped with body armor. They shared with the Army beginning in March 1952, when each Army division was given 350 of the "Marine vests" to use on patrols. The Army quickly began to request more between August 1952 and March 1953, reaching up to 63,000 until finally standardizing their own armor.

While several thousand of the World War II-era M12 armor vests existed in supply, they were not issued until after such studies proved their effectiveness and sparked interest, and stocks were quickly exhausted. The older-style vest used aluminum plates inserted in a nylon vest, which resulted in a paneling effect. It was nearly twice as heavy as its Marine Corps counterpart, was covered in snaps and straps, and was generally uncomfortable compared to the new models. Nevertheless, it was the dominant vest issued to Army personnel before the Marine Corps-type vest became available.

The Army T1952 vest was all nylon with an exterior fabric of vinyl-coated nylon poncho material, which had a tendency to shine and reflect light. Over the ribs and shoulder was a layer of sponge rubber for comfort and shock absorption. Two pockets on the front of the vest closed with a concealed snap and three dot-snaps secured the front. The full vest extended lower and covered more of the torso than the M12 vest. It also included four nylon loops around the bottom to help suspend cartridge or pistol belts.

Only after extensive testing and troubles with contracts and manufacturing was the Army able to produce its M1952 nylon vest, which rivaled the Marine Corps vest in function and comfort. It began as the third revision of the T1952 with improvements of a nylon covering, lace-up sides for adjustment and expansion, zip-up front with snap fly, improvements to the interior nylon layers, and web straps on the chest for carrying grenades. These vests left the United States in December 1952 and began to arrive in theater by February 1953 in limited numbers while combat units were instructed to make use of their existing stocks.

The M1952 vests had an immense psychological effect on the wearers when in action. Physically, they tended not to notice the weight or any excessive heat, though removing the vest after wear in summer heat typically revealed saturated fatigues. The effect on confidence was measurable and for a limited war in which fighting men often became cautious, the introduction of body armor reinvigorated a sense of motivation and aggressiveness.

A better example of the T1952 vest shows snap and strap details and most importantly the nylon material, which appears dark and shiny like a satin finish. (US National Museum of Health and Medicine KWB 53-2511-171)

SPECIAL UNIFORMS

Many Army troops, particularly drivers and those in armored units, used M1944 goggles extensively to combat the endemic dust during dry periods of the summer season – the only period of the Korean War in which they can be seen used in such numbers, due to the mobile nature of combat. Following the transition to more static warfare, the need apparently dwindled, leaving the summer of 1950 as the high point of use for goggles.

This group of tankers all wear M1944 goggles and M1943 soft caps; note the soldier at left with the cap's earflaps down. (Author's Collection)

Despite their flying status, Army aviators could still be considered to be ground troops as they were predominantly artillery officers in field-artillery battalions. They were among the most diverse among their ranks in terms of combat uniform choices and were characterized by their use of aviator sunglasses. Depending on the season and type of aircraft, aviators employed several types of flyers' jackets or flight suits recognizable from Air Force (or previously Army Air Force) stocks. Leather bomber-style jackets were also a common choice and often garnished with shoulder holsters.

Tankers maintained use of the M1938 "Rawlings" helmet, often in tandem with the M1944 goggles. Developed and patented by the Rawlings Manufacturing Company, the helmet was manufactured by other companies as well under the simple nomenclature "Tank Helmet." The helmet was made of hard fiber resin with a leather suspension and leather earflaps. A variety of web and leather straps with snaps offered adjustment and security to the wearer. Headset receivers and microphones were both integrated into the design and their cords and cables may be seen hanging out and around the helmet when in operation.

Armored troops were also issued with the classic "tanker jacket." The second pattern with slash pockets was dominant, but the author has noted several instances of the scarce first-pattern jacket with patch pockets being worn in Korea as well. The garment, actually known as "Jacket, Combat, Winter," became associated with armored troops after it was issued to them to supplement their lack of cold-weather gear in unheated vehicles. It had an OD No. 3 cotton outer with wool lining, elastic cuffs and collar, and a zip-up front. The stylish and functional jacket was coveted by all troops and, by the Korean War era, had inspired many tailored and privately purchased models.

There existed many common practices for certain occupations and personalities, particularly among high-ranking staff and general officers who had their own particular styles and accouterments. Many used equipment retained from prewar service, including M1936 suspenders, tanker jackets, B15 jackets, and other exclusive, custom, or uncommon items.

This fine example of the "Shirt, Field, Wool, Olive Green Shade 108" features full-color insignia, locally made nametape, and detailed cross-stitching. Of interest is the very late use of the small M1948 chevrons. The "Shirt, Field, Wool, Olive Green Shade 108" was designed and adopted early in the Korean War, but not issued until late in the conflict. It was significantly thicker than its predecessors, with a wide "butterfly" collar, low pockets, and unusual stitching for the shoulder panel that put an angled seam across the collarbone. Period photographs show use of the shirt in what could be the winter of 1952/53, but with insufficient quantities to issue until after the armistice the shirt was not worn until the winter of 1953/54. The "Trousers, Field, Wool, M1951" were a wool–nylon serge blend and noticeably darker and greener than any previous wools. The design was similar to the M1943 cotton field trousers, including adjustment tabs with slide buckles at the waist. These did not arrive in Korea before the end of hostilities. (Author's Collection)

INSIGNIA

The use of all insignia allowed the Marine with his Eagle, Globe, and Anchor insignia and the soldier with his colorful array of personal and unit badges to display enormous pride in himself and his unit. The practice of adding insignia to the helmet was almost as prevalent as it was during World War II. The nicknames, lore, and comradery built up from months in combat led everyone to claim their unit was the best in Korea.

Rank insignia

Both Army and Marine Corps enlisted men frequently adopted theater-made chevrons for wear on headgear. These were of heavy brass construction sand-cast from melted-down bullet and shell casings scavenged from the battlefield. Army chevrons were painted with a blue background to match the M1951 chevrons; Marines used red. Chevrons were most frequently worn on soft caps and pile caps fixed by crude screw-post backings. The small M1948 chevrons were also a popular choice for wear on soft caps because of their smaller size – perhaps the one advantage to what was widely considered an ugly and unpopular chevron.

Officers frequently had at least their rank insignia on the front of the helmet, whether it was painted or brazed on. Enlisted men added chevrons to a lesser extent, but all ranks from private first class through first sergeant are noted to have done so. The leadership stripe to indicate officer or noncommissioned officer status was still used and was still not made to any specific regulation, resulting in a range of dimensions deviating from the suggested 1×4in bar.

OPPOSITE
This lieutenant is one of several of the 140th Tank Battalion, 40th Infantry Division, who were apparently issued the first-pattern winter combat "tanker jacket." The collection of images from the unit includes several examples of the early jacket in use alongside the more recognizable second pattern. Though his jacket is blowing open, it is among the clearer images of the jacket to show the patch pocket. In addition to the jacket, he wears the M1945 HBT jacket and trousers, five-button sweater, double-buckle boots, leather gloves, and M1943 cap with rank insignia. (Author's Collection)

The heavy brass theater-made chevrons used by both Army and Marines are shown in detail and as originally worn on a theater-made M1943-type cap and a pile cap. There are many variations of size, quality, and colors. (Author's Collection)

This typical arrangement of officers' insignia on the field uniform shows metal rank badges soldered to the helmet and collar insignia indicating the officer's rank of major and his branch of service, the artillery. The artillery crossed cannons include "52" for the 52d Field Artillery Battalion. (Author's Collection)

Despite general disdain for the M1948 chevrons, they were issued and within regulation and therefore widely worn in Korea across all field uniforms. At the time they were introduced, however, the Army revised its rank structure to omit the three-stripe sergeant insignia, which was a controversy on top of the insignia revision. To compound this, the Army decided to distinguish between combat and non-combat troops by creating two colorways: blue on a yellow background for combat and yellow on blue for non-combat. This led to bitter resentment by those who fell into the "non-combat" occupational specialty series. Many soldiers of "non-combat" units became sarcastic and cynical about the insignia when they inevitably came under fire and debated how to get their sewing kits and quickly swap over their chevrons.

Enlisted men continued to wear old-stock chevrons (either to use up supply or avoid the M1948 chevrons) and Japanese-made chevrons. The latter mimicked the rayon-on-blue twill chevrons of World War II, but the rayon/silk embroidered thread was bright white and silvery and the cotton twill backing was black.

The introduction of M1951 embroidered green-on-blue twill chevrons resolved some of the problems that arose from the M1948 type, but did not completely replace them by the end of the Korean War, and it was just another style added into the mix of insignia. This new pattern reverted to the original size and omitted the distinguishing colors between combat or non-combat troops, but there was no change to rank structure and the plain three-stripe sergeant insignia was never produced or worn.

In the field, the Marine Corps continued to stencil enlisted rank insignia. Officers could wear pin-on collar rank insignia. Similarly, Army officers wore their rank and branch insignia on the collar. Numbered brass denoting infantry regiment or artillery battalion continued to be very popular. Metal pin-on and sewn fabric rank insignia was used on field-jacket shoulder loops, the fabric insignia sometimes ingeniously created from found material such as white underwear drawstrings to create bars.

This fantastic display of insignia includes four types of chevrons. From left to right, beginning with the two soldiers sitting on the vehicle, we see a small M1948 chevron denoting a private first class and what appears to be a Japanese-made bright-white black-edged chevron. Below are a corporal and sergeant wearing M1951 chevrons and another private first class with a small M1948 chevron. This photograph was taken no earlier than 1953 and shows the variety of insignia still used at that time despite updates and regulations. Note the mix of HBTs and field jackets as well as the use of jump wings on all caps that have some degree of stiffeners. (Author's Collection)

Nametapes

The nametape became standardized among some Army units and the Marines likewise employed stamped names above the left breast pocket. These were in the typical Navy and Marine Corps style of initials with surname in simple, Sans Serif font. After July 1953 and possibly in the later months of the Korean War, the Marines did begin to use theater-made embroidered-on-white tapes. These often included the Marine's name in Hangul (Korean).

The Army nametape, typically a simple strip of heavy canvas-like fabric in white with a stamped surname only, was also worn above the left breast pocket. As usual, many variations existed within the Army and there was no standard for color or dimensions.

Special embroidered nametapes surfaced as well, including branch colors and multiple lines to include occupation or translated name

This pair of uniforms from an engineer officer of the 40th Infantry Division shows an officer's wool shirt with brightly colored nametape as well as his 1947-type HBT shirt (see p.5) with a much more subdued nametape. Of interest is the "Ball of Fire" lozenge-shaped insignia used by the division only in Korea. (Author's Collection)

41

The more refined field uniform for honor-guard duty is embellished here with a polished helmet with large regimental insignia on the front. The glare obscures the 31st Infantry Regiment's polar bear insignia, which covers most of the crown of the helmet. Farther from the front, more white canvas might appear in leggings, gloves, ascots, and shoulder cords; even chromed helmets could be used. The pistol belt is dyed darker, similar to the forest-green type with the large flat brass clasp, but this belt retains the standard buckle, though it too has been polished along with the other metal components. This soldier also wears an ascot of infantry blue. Note the M1945 HBT jacket with added shoulder loops and sleeve pockets. A pipe protrudes from the left sleeve near the 7th Infantry Division insignia. (Author's Collection)

in Hangul. Some units embraced their heritage, particularly the 17th Infantry Regiment, which had white-on-blue nametapes with a silhouette of a buffalo above the wearer's name.

Unit insignia

Men of all Army units wore their divisional, corps, or army patches mounted on the upper left sleeve both in reserve and in combat. Despite these being potentially bright targets, the threat seemed negligible due to the patches' high volume of use as the Korean War progressed. While the majority of these patches were of standard manufacture, there were occurrences of theater-made examples and variations exclusive to the Korean campaign. Patches worn on dress uniforms included an even greater variety of styles, color, construction, and accompanying tabs and scrolls, but as the subject of this text is the field uniform, it should be noted that there were far fewer deviations from the standard-issue patches.

An example of a variant that was widely adopted for the field uniform was the 40th Infantry Division's "Ball of Fire" patch, which could include a scroll bearing the nickname. The normally blue square diamond was stretched into a lozenge shape with the sunburst elongated to match and embellished by the addition of a red center burning out to orange and yellow. This was proudly displayed on the divisional signboard, so it was apparently acceptable to higher ranks who would normally discourage the use of unauthorized insignia.

Many armored battalions wore their numbered triangle above the pocket in addition to divisional insignia on the sleeve. The practice of wearing the armored triangle on the chest dates back to World War II; the reasons are unclear, beyond legends associated with General George S. Patton. Men of the 40th Infantry Division also had an interesting practice of wearing their insignia over the pocket on the left side of the chest.

The 187th Regimental Combat Team (Airborne) initially wore the 11th Airborne Division patch, but later adopted its own design for the regiment as it maintained independent status. The 5th Regimental Combat Team similarly had its own insignia. All other units predominantly wore the patch of their parent unit. Airborne Ranger companies were authorized to wear the new yellow-on-black Ranger tab, but many adapted World War II Ranger battalion scrolls by picking out "Bn" and re-stitching "Co."

Unit insignia on helmets did seem to have some standardization where the divisional insignia was painted or decaled on one side of the shell and regimental insignia on the other. In reviewing thousands of photographs, the 2d and 24th Infantry divisions appear most frequently with decorated helmets, but the 1st Cavalry Division almost never so.

The 2d Infantry Division retained its practice of placing insignia on the front of the helmet. For garrison and honor guards, some units placed their regimental insignia on the front as well. The 187th Regimental Combat Team (Airborne) used large half-circle tactical markings on each side of the helmet. These were sectioned to indicate battalion. A solid half-circle indicated regimental headquarters; one division indicated the 1st Battalion, two for the 2d Battalion, and three for the 3d Battalion. This was a practice carried over from the regimental tactical markings made famous by paratrooper units of World War II. Most photos of the 187th in combat display these large and rather conspicuous markings.

Combat badges

Ever a source of pride, the Army's Combat Infantryman Badge was resented by other branches, particularly the artillery, who continued to feel slighted as they were subject to the same harrowing conditions as infantrymen. Forward observers especially sought ways to display their combat service, resulting in increasing numbers of unauthorized badges during the Korean War.

The combat artillery badge is the only one known to have been created and worn in theater using repainted or recast Combat Infantryman badges with crossed cannons applied over or in place of the rifle. This gave rise to similar combat badges for the other services. In the years following the Korean War, one particular manufacturer created anodized badges for combat artillery, combat armor/armored cavalry, and possibly others, but these are the only two types known to the author to have been worn on dress uniforms. Army Pamphlet PAM20-158, published in March 1953, notes the Combat Artillery and Armor badges as unauthorized badges that could subject the wearer to a fine of up to $250, imprisonment up to six months, or both. Despite the potential consequences, the proud GI flagrantly ignored these strictures.

Proudly worn by forward observers in the artillery, ascots were on occasion issued to units regardless of their branch affiliation, as a tactical signifier; while paratroopers adopted camouflage silk ascots made from parachute material, members of the 3d Ranger Company fashioned their own out of midnight-black silk. These four ascots in the author's collection are known to date from the Korean War period. From left to right: a plain white silk ascot with ties shows a very small embroidered 24th Infantry Division insignia; a standard infantry-blue rayon ascot of significant length, meant to be wrapped and tucked around the neck for a billowing appearance; a bright-red silk 40th Infantry Division ascot; and a scarlet 981st Field Artillery Battalion ascot featuring a hand-embroidered unit number and crossed cannons, unrelated, but coincidentally a unit organic to the 40th Infantry Division. (Author's Collection)

An array of artillerymen in the later stages of the Korean War pose in front of a sandbag bunker. Note the rank and unit insignia, name tags, and the officer (near center, sitting) wearing the 7th Infantry Division's Order of the Bayonet badge. (Author's Collection)

BIBLIOGRAPHY

Andrews, Lisa Anne Neil (2020). *Peter Howland Monfore: Letters From Korea*. Tukwila, WA: Blurb, Inc.

Appleman, Roy E. (1987). *East of Chosin.* College Station, TX: Texas A&M University Press.

Channon, Robert I. (1993). *The Cold Steel Third: Third Airborne Ranger Company 1950–51.* Franklin, NC: Genealogy Publishing Service.

Dill, James Hamilton (1993). *16 Days at Mungol-Li.* Fayetteville, AR: M&M Press.

Dill, James H. (n.d.). "Personal Adventures Inchon–Seoul 1950." Manuscript, undated.

Drozd, Joseph J. (n.d.). "My Baptism of Fire." Manuscript, undated.

Drozd, Joseph J. (n.d.). "The Battle of Chochiwon." Manuscript, undated.

Drozd, Joseph J. (n.d.). "The Naktong River Crossing and Hill #1157." Manuscript, undated.

Ent, Uzal W. (2010). *Breakout: Defense of the Pusan Perimeter*. Harrisburg, PA: Stackpole Books.

Francois, Gerard (n.d.). "Jerry Francois Memoirs." Charmaine Francois-Griffith, undated.

Hallahan, Robert F. (2003). *All Good Men: A Lieutenant's Memoir of the Korean War.* Bloomington, IN: iUniverse.

Harrity, Ralph Derr (2005). *Q Clan: The First Summer of the Korean Conflict, June–September 1950, a Lieutenant's Memoir.* Pittsburgh, PA: Dorrance Publishing Co.

Holliday, Sam (2014). *Forgotten.* Tarentum, PA: Word Association Publishers.

Holt, Robert J. (2006–23). "Tank Helmet M-1938 & Related Equipment." http://www.752tank.com/TankHelmet.html (accessed July 5, 2023).

Mackowiak, Robert C. (2005–21). Personal Interviews with Carlos Coleman, Robert L. Quintal, Sr., Anthony Torsiello, and John Considine.

McMaster, George (2001). "Memoir of George McMaster." Korean War Educator. http://www.koreanwar-educator.org/memoirs/mcmaster_george/index.htm (accessed July 5, 2023).

Meid, Pat (Lieutenant Colonel, USMCR) & James M. Yingling (Major, USMC) (1972). *U.S. Marine Operations in Korea 1950—1953 Volume V: Operations in West Korea.* Washington, DC: Historical Division, Headquarters, US Marine Corps.

Montross, Lynn & Nicholas A. Canzona (1953). *The Pusan Perimeter: U.S. Marine Operations in Korea, 1950–1953, vol. 1.*

Montross, Lynn & Nicholas A. Canzona (1955). *The Inchon-Seoul Operation: U.S. Marine Operations in Korea, 1950–1953, vol. 2.*

Montross, Lynn & Nicholas A. Canzona (1957). *The Chosin Reservoir Campaign: U.S. Marine Operations in Korea, 1950–1953, vol. 3.*

Montross, Lynn, Hubard D. Kuokka (Maj, USMC), & Norman W. Hicks (Maj, USMC) (1962). *The East–Central Front: U.S. Marine Operations in Korea, 1950–1953, vol. 4.*

Rasula, George (1950). "Before the Deployment: In Japan." The New York Military Affairs Symposium.

US Army Medical Service (1962). "Medical Department, Army: Wound Ballistics."

Interview with Captain Edward P. Stamford. Historical Division: Headquarters, US Marine Corps, 1951.

PLATE COMMENTARIES

A: THE WAR BEGINS, SUMMER 1950
A1: Private, 24th Infantry Division, summer 1950
This young soldier is tired and hungry, and has just been resupplied with .30-caliber rifle ammunition. He is an example of the first US troops deployed from Japan to combat the North Korean assault from the north. His uniform, once clean, with polished boots and emblazoned helmet, is now filthy, on the verge of wearing through, and impregnated with several days of sweat. The unit-marked helmets – some with a glossy finish – were issued out of necessity, but the practice became accepted and embraced during the Korean War.

A2: Staff Sergeant, 1st Provisional Marine Brigade, August 1950
The 1st Provisional Marine Brigade assembled rapidly around the 5th Marine Regiment and arrived directly from the United States as a temporary solution to get the Marine Corps into Korea as quickly as possible. Despite embarkation orders listing the camouflage helmet cover accompanying the steel helmet, it seems all Marines of the brigade had only the bare steel helmet. Armed with an M2 Carbine, this Marine shows the practice of stenciled chevrons to indicate his rank of staff sergeant. The Marines immediately earned a reputation among the North Korean units they faced, which recognized them by their distinctive khaki leggings.

A3: Private, 1st Marine Division, September 1950
Upon formation of the 1st Marine Division, the hard-fought 1st Provisional Marine Brigade was absorbed into the division, which became complete in time for the amphibious landing at Inchon. Each of the assault troops carried one 'Food Packet, Individual Assault, 1A1' and two canteens of water for provisions among their equipment. Packs, shelter-halves, and entrenching tools remained part of the combat load throughout the operation and the helmet cover exclusive to the Marine Corps was issued once again.

B: MOBILE WARFARE, LATE 1950
B1: Corporal, 1st Cavalry Division, October 1950
US troops chased North Korean forces up and down the western front of Korea from summer through winter. Near the end of winter, the men of the 1st Cavalry Division had been in near-constant combat for months amid challenging and abrasive terrain. A wet winter made the troops constantly damp, dirty, and cold. A heavy load was common as men carried all of their belongings with them. Many had disposed of their helmets in favor of soft caps, particularly the pile cap, which was lighter, quieter, and warmer. This man wears his rank of corporal on the brim of his hat – a rank he likely earned quickly to replenish the ranks of the fallen.

B2: Lieutenant Colonel, 7th Infantry Division, November 1950

This officer of the 7th Infantry Division is inspired by the commanders who led the doomed battalions of the 31st Regimental Combat Team on the east side of the Chosin Reservoir. His clothing is barely adequate for the climate and beneath the bulky parka he has layered nearly every piece of uniform he owns. He is among the fortunate few to have proper mittens, but they are often left dangling around his neck.

B3: Private, 1st Marine Division, December 1950

The Marines who fought out their entrapment on the west side of the Chosin Reservoir hardly fared better than the Army units, which were severely attrited by waves of Chinese troops. For several days and nights, the US troops fought without respite. Many of the wounded remained fighting – in many cases their wounds congealed due to the cold, which saved their lives. By the end, they were unshaven, exhausted, and detached from reality. In the subzero temperatures, the Marine winter uniform was reasonably adequate, though bulky, and shoepacs were an advantage over regular leather boots.

C: SPRING 1951

C1: Private, 187th Airborne Regimental Combat Team (Airborne), May 1951

In Korea, only the 187th Regimental Combat Team (Airborne) was deployed, despite an entire division being suggested, and it seemed every stateside paratrooper was eager to fight. They participated in two combat jumps – one in May 1951, in which this trooper has just participated. The unit carried over the custom of distinguishing markings on the helmet to identify men at battalion level; this soldier belongs to the 2d Battalion. He also wears "rigger"-modified trousers with large pockets for carrying extra equipment and is generously supplied with ammunition.

C2: Corporal, 3d Airborne Ranger Company, 3d Infantry Division, April 1951

Even more rambunctious than the airborne troops were the Airborne Rangers. Each infantry division was allotted one company – this subject being of the 3d Airborne Ranger Company of the 3d Infantry Division. Known as the "Cold Steel Third" for their use of the bayonet, this company is possibly the best-documented of the Rangers in Korea and included many colorful characters that inspired this particular Ranger. He is an assistant BAR-man (one of two in a Ranger squad given an additional BAR versus a regular infantry squad) and carries the respective ammunition belt with rifle ammunition carried in bandoleers. On his suspenders hang two white-phosphorous grenades, which seemed to have been a favored weapon within the company. He proudly displays a "Ranger" tab over his divisional insignia.

C3: Sergeant, 2d Infantry Division, spring 1951

The Korean War saw the end of segregation in the US Army, but not without a few all-Black battalions in the first year of the war. The 3d Battalion, 9th Infantry Regiment, was one of them and this sergeant of the heavy-weapons company has shouldered his recoilless rifle to take aim. His kit is similar to that of any infantryman with the addition of the M2 ammunition vest, which could hold rocket, mortar, or recoilless-rifle rounds. He wears no insignia except for the divisional symbol painted on the front of his helmet.

D: 1951–52

D1: Lieutenant, artillery, 25th Infantry Division, autumn 1951

Artillery officers tended to be very intelligent and sensitive to their surroundings. Many of them wrote extensive memoirs of their experiences. This individual of the 25th Infantry Division is an amalgamation of many of these young officers who served as forward observers and liaison officers to infantry units. They entered bitter fights at the front rather than remaining in the relative safety of fire-direction centers and gun batteries. Many proudly wore the crossed cannons and scarlet ascot to distinguish them as artillerymen as they were otherwise identical in appearance to the average infantryman.

D2: Private first class, field artillery, summer 1951

Supporting the calls for fire missions from observers were the hard-working artillery gunners loading and firing shells with the efficiency of machines. In Korea's sweltering summer heat, they often shed their equipment, jackets, and shirts.

D3: Private, 40th Infantry Division, February 1952

At the beginning of 1952, the 40th and 45th Infantry divisions rotated to Korea from Japan. Fresh National Guard troops arrived as whole units and wore relatively clean and adequate equipment. This automatic rifleman has not yet experienced combat and has only been patrolling the snowcapped hills. He wears his pile cap under his helmet with the earflaps down over his ears. He needs only the pile liner for warmth – this also allows for easier movement with his heavy weapon and equipment load – and leather work gloves. He will soon experience numerous skirmishes in the outpost battles.

E: BODY ARMOR AND BEHIND THE LINES, 1952

E1: Sergeant, 1st Marine Division, spring 1952

The Marine shown here exhibits the early standardization of the flak vest, an article of armor that became an integral part of the combat uniform. He is neat in appearance with well-

Master Sergeant Clifford R. Rodriguez of the 187th Regimental Combat Team (Airborne) receives a decoration from Brigadier General Frank S. Bowen in February 1951. Rodriguez wears the new M1951 pile cap with plain brim. Note also his use of 11th Airborne Division shoulder insignia and the master sergeant chevrons on his M1943 jacket. Bowen wears the older M1943 or MQ1 pile cap and has sewn brigadier stars onto the shoulder loops of his field jacket. (US Signal Corps Photo #SC-358677)

Major General Henry I. Hodes, depicted during his brief period commanding the 24th Infantry Division, wears a very crisp, clean M1943 uniform set. The jacket is dark in color and exhibits the sateen sheen of fresh material. He wears shoepacs, a pile liner under his field jacket, and a soft cap under his helmet, and also appears to use silk parachute material as a scarf. Note the bare loops of his helmet where the chinstraps have been removed. (Signal Corps Photo #SC-393159)

fitting utilities and manages to stay groomed, but is unable to eradicate the dirt and dust from his skin and clothing. By 1952 the war was fought from bunkers and trenches that gave inhabitants a sense of home while they were on the line. He wears the fairly new lace-up Marine combat boots that slowly replaced the old leggings and boondockers. It was a major change for the Marine Corps that had so much pride in its distinctive customs, but like the flak vest the adoption of boots was a sign of the advances in modern warfare.

E2: Soldier, infantry, summer 1952
This soldier wears the Army-type M12 flak vest and its myriad of armor panels. The bulky vest inhibits comfortable and efficient carrying of equipment, so his cartridge belt hangs low over his hips. He carries grenades to repel uphill attacks by assaulting Chinese troops. The author has seen many photographs of soldiers with several grenades hanging from all affordances on vests, belts, and even rifle slings, but suspects such displays are for the sake of the photograph. It is more reasonable that only a few grenades would be carried at a time and any additional grenades would be used directly out of shipping crates to roll down the steep hillsides.

E3: Private first class, 17th Infantry Regiment, 7th Infantry Division, 1952
A soldier in reserve displays the professional and colorful appearance made popular during the Korean War. He has had local tailors modify his fatigues for better fit and added

sleeve pockets and shoulder loops that contrast with the different shade and wear of the shirt. On his left chest he wears a blue nametape with a silhouette of a buffalo that was exclusive to the 17th Infantry Regiment. Above this is his Combat Infantryman Badge. Sewn on his sleeve pocket is the small private first class chevron and his 7th Infantry Division patch. He has had the opportunity to polish his boots and neatly blouses his trousers over them with the help of inserts such as spring loops to maintain shape.

F: POSITIONAL WARFARE, 1952–53
F1: Private, a replacement company, winter 1952
A new replacement soldier smiles despite the winter chill – he does not yet know what he is getting into. He may be on sentry duty, in reserve, or passing through the pipeline to his assigned unit, so stands casually with only his rifle and winter clothing. He is equipped with the heavy M1948 parka and a new pair of M1951 trousers, both of which are worn atop plenty of other layers of clothing. His hands and feet stay warm in gauntlet-type mittens and "Mickey Mouse" boots.

F2: Sergeant, 5th Regimental Combat Team, 1953
With the burlap helmet cover and Marine-type flak vest, this soldier portrays an iconic image of the Korean War infantryman. The soldier of 1953 was far detached from the early days of campaigning and passed the days in sturdy bunkers and trenches of heavy log and sandbag construction. He wears his armor vest unzipped as he has become nonchalant after only a few weeks in combat, but also because it is too tight when zipped securely. The wool shirt is a popular choice at the time in lieu of the HBT jacket; the wool is breathable and blends in with dusty surroundings. His trousers are rolled over his boots. He carries only his carbine with two 30-round magazines taped together and a few grenades from his flak vest.

F3: Brigadier general, IX Corps, 1952
This brigadier general is an older soldier who has been in the Army for some considerable time. He is nearly 50 years old and has held every command up to his present assignment of an assistant division commander. As he does little fighting anymore, he is clean and his uniform is pressed. He has acquired a B15-type jacket for wear in the cold months and carries only a pistol in a shoulder holster.

G: IN THE FIELD, 1952–53
G1: First sergeant, 45th Infantry Division, 1953
This "old man" rivaling the senior officers in age and experience is only in his mid- to late forties, but has aged significantly during his years as an infantryman. A supply sergeant or field first sergeant, he is not shy about displaying his senior noncommissioned rank of first sergeant, which is boldly painted on his helmet. On his sleeves, he also wears the small M1948 chevrons and proudly displays his current divisional insignia as well as his World War II combat unit on his right sleeve. As his duties revolve around support of his officers and men, and effectively running a company, he carries little equipment other than a pistol.

G2: Sergeant first class, engineer combat battalion, 1952
This engineer is easy to recognize because of his mine detector. He also carries a full cartridge belt and rifle. He wears a theater-made field jacket inspired by one in the author's collection worn by a combat engineer. Styled after the M1941 jacket, it is short in length for easy movement and has additional

sleeve pockets. On his chest, he wears a locally made nametape of somewhat crude construction. His use of the small M1948 chevrons shows they are still circulating and used, even though the new chevrons were beginning to replace them, especially on field jackets.

G3: Private first class, medical company, 1952
The one piece of equipment to indicate combat medics during the Korean War was their large medical kit bag. This young soldier is a draftee with no inclination for the medical field, but a short course for medical aidmen was sufficient by Army standards to get him into combat. This particular medic is evidently proud of his rank and has decorated his helmet with a simple private first class chevron. He also wears a Combat Medical Badge above his left pocket – the only other indication of his occupational specialty. He carries a carbine and only a few magazines for defense against Chinese troops, who did not recognize the articles of the Geneva Convention.

H: SPECIALISTS, 1953
H1: Captain, aviation detachment, 1953
While pilots may not be considered ground troops, their service within Army units warrants their inclusion. Artillery and engineers used them as observers and each regiment adopted

Major Jack J. Kron, an artillery officer, wears a field overcoat, the M1943 field cap with metal rank insignia, and leather gloves. He carries on his pistol belt a knife or M4 bayonet, compass, pistol-magazine pouch, and first-aid kit. (Author's Collection)

aviation companies for such roles as well as liaison pilots. They became an integral part of the infantry division. Their work uniforms vary significantly from typical Army troops as they were supplied from Air Force or old Army Air Force stock. They wore summer- or winter-weight flight suits of all patterns. This pilot displays his wings and rank on his baseball-type cap. His only weapon is a pistol in a shoulder holster.

H2: Sergeant, tank battalion, 1953
This tanker shows the standard outfit for an armored soldier. His fiber helmet, "tanker jacket," and goggles set him apart from other ground troops when he is not in his tank. His face is soiled from dusty roads except for the clean outline from his goggles. This is likely due to road movement or an armored infantry patrol as tanks were predominantly dug into pits by mid- to late war. He stands casually with his jacket unzipped and an M3 submachine gun. As the tank commander, he holds the rank of sergeant and wears the large-type chevrons on his sleeves.

H3: Private, military police, Eighth US Army, 1953
While many military policemen in Korea were assigned to traffic duties, it is easy to overlook the danger of their occupation when only a few men were posted to an intersection in the wilderness with the threat of guerrillas and infiltrators rampant. Military police always wore their brassards and were also equipped with a matching slip-on sleeve for the brim of the pile cap during the winter months. Army MPs used a white font on a black background and Marines wore their gold on red. Leather belts and pouches, whistles, and lanyards were additional distinguishing items for MPs depending on their proximity to combat. For ceremonial-type duties and responsibilities farther from the front, they had more freedom to display a clean and flashy uniform. His helmet is glossy and emblazoned with large bright banding and insignia for "MP" and Eighth US Army. His open collar shows a green ascot of the military police branch color. A whistle chain is looped up into his pocket and there is a white nametape above his chest pocket. His web gear deviates from the norm as his pistol belt has been modified with a large brass plate fastener that he keeps at a high polish; the fabric has been dyed a dark forest green. His pistol-magazine pouch is brown leather to match his holster.

Army officers just before their fight east of Chosin, November 12, 1950. At left, 31st Infantry Regiment commander Colonel Allan D. MacLean and 3d Battalion commander Colonel William R. Reilly. MacLean wears the M1943 field uniform with 31st Infantry Regiment insignia on shoulder loops; he also wears M1936 suspenders and leather gloves. Reilly wears the anorak common to the 7th Infantry Division during the period; note his Marine Corps camouflage cover "acquired" at some point between the Inchon landing and the advance into North Korea. On the right is X Corps commander Major General Edward M. Almond wearing a winter combat jacket, wool trousers, and M1943 cap. Note his general stars directly embroidered onto the field-jacket shoulders. The fourth man's identity has not been established. (US Signal Corps Photo #SC-352539)

INDEX

References to illustration captions are shown in **bold**. Plates are shown with page and caption locators in brackets.

Almond, Maj. Gen. Edward M. **47**

ammunition, means of carrying 34, 36, 45: bags 34; bandoleers 22, **A1**(25, 44), **C1–2**(27, 45), 34, **35**, **36**; belts **23**, **24**, **C2**(27, 45), **E2**(29, 46), **G2**(31, 46–47), 33, 35, **36**, 37; boxes 34; clips 24, **A1**(25, 44), 35; magazines **F2**(30, 46), **G3**(31, 47), 33; pouches 33; vests **C3**(27, 45), 34

anoraks/parkas 11, 14, 18–19, 20, **20**, 21, **21**, 22, **B2**(26, 45), **F1**(30, 46), **47**

armies: Eighth 11, 15, **39**, **H3**(32, 47)

armor vests **E1–2**(29, 45–46), **F2**(30, 46), 33, 37, **37**

armored battalions (Army) 17, 38

armored divisions (Army): 11th 42, **45**

artillery forces (Army) 9, 20, 22, **23**, **D2**(28, 45), 38, 40, **40**, **43**, 43, 47, **47**

ascots **D1**(28, 45), **H3**(32, 47), **42**, 43

automatic (BAR) riflemen **C2**(27, 45), **D3**(28, 45), **24**, 33

aviators 9, 12, **H1**(32, 47), 38, 47

badges/decorations/wings 5, 12, **E3**(29, 46), **G3**(31, 47), **H1**(32, 47), **41**, 43, **43**, 45

bayonets 24, **24**, **C2**(27, 45), 33, 35, **35**, **36**, **47**

bedrolls/blankets/sleeping bags 19, 35

belts **3**, 6, **6**, **9**, **15**, 19, 20, 22, **24**, **A2**(25, 44), **G1**, **3**(31, 46–47), **H3**(32, 47), 34, **36**, **38**, **43**

binoculars **B2**(26, 45), **D1**(28, 45), 34

"boondockers" (shoes) **3**, **7**, 14, 46

boots **3**, 5, **6**, **7**, **8**, **9**, **10**, 13–14, **13**, **14**, 16, 19, **19**, **20**, **24**, **A1–B2**(25–26, 44–45), **C1–G3**(27–31, 45–47), **H2–3**(32, 47), **38**, 41, **43**

Bowen, Brig. Gen. Frank S. **45**

buttons/snaps 4, 6, 7, 9, 15, 20, 21, 22, 33, 34, 35, 37, 38

caps **3**, **7**, **9**, 10, **10**, 11, **13**, **14**, **17**, 22, **24**, **D2**(28, 45), **H1**(32, 47), 38, 39, 41, **46**, 47, **47**: pile caps 11–12, **11**, **12**, 16, 18, 21, **B1**(26, 44), **D3**(28, 45), **F1**(30, 46), 39, **40**, **45**, 47; Ridgway Cap 10–11, **17**, **E2**(29, 46)

cavalry divisions (Army): 1st **B1**(26, 44), 42

cold-weather/winter attire **7**, 10, 11–12, 14, 15–22, **19**, **20**, **21**, **22**, **B1–3**(26, 44–45), **F1**(30, 46), 38, **38**, **47**

collar insignia 5, 40, **40**, **D1**(28, 45)

compasses 34, **47**

corps (Army): IX **F3**(30, 46); X **47**

coveralls/overalls/utilities 4, 6–7, **6**, **E1**(29, 45–46)

engineer combat battalions **G2**(31, 46–47)

engineers 20, **G2**(31, 46–47), 47

equipment/gear/kit **3**, 6, **6**, **7**, **7**, **9**, **15**, **16**, 19, **19**, 20, 21, 22, 23–24, **23**, **24**, **A1–3**(25, 44), **B2–C3**(26–27, 45), **D1**, **3**(28, 45), **E2**(29, 46), **F2–H3**(30–32, 46–47), 33, **33**, 34, **34**, 35–36, **35**, **36**, 37, **38**, **38**, **42**, **43**, 45, **47**

fatigues 4, 19, **E3**(29, 46), 37

field artillery battalions (Army) 38: 52d **23**, 40; 981st **43**

flight suits **H1**(32, 47), 38

forward observers 43

gloves 19, 22, **22**, **C3**(27, 45), **D2–3**(28, 45), **H2**(32, 47), **38**, **42**, **47**

goggles 38, **38**

grenades 24, **C2**(27, 45), **E2**(29, 46), **F2**(30, 46), 34, 37

heavy-weapons companies (Army) **C3**(27, 45)

helmet covers/nets 6, 8, 23, **23**, **A2–3**(25, 44), **E1**(29, 45–46), **36**

helmet liners/shells 23, 34

helmets **3**, 6, 8, 10, 11, 12, **13**, 19, 20, 23, **24**, **A2**(25, 44), **C2**(27, 45), **D3**(28, 45), **E2**(29, 46), **F1**(30, 46), **H2**(32, 47), 33, 34, **36**, 37, 38, **38**, **42**, 46: insignia on 8, 14, 15, 23, **A1**(25, 44), **B2**(26, 45), **C1**, **3**(27, 45), **D1**(28, 45), **F3–G3**(30–31, 46–47), **H3**(32, 47), 33, 39, **40**, 42, **42**, 46

Henderson, Col. Frederick P. **7**

Hodes, Maj. Gen. Henry I. **46**

honor guards 42, **42**

infantry divisions (Army) 45, 47: 2d 9, **16**, **C3**(27, 45), 42; 3d 12, 24, **24**, **C2**(27, 45), 42, 43, **47**; 7th **15**, 16, 17, 20, 21, 22, **B2**(26, 45), **E3**(29, 46), 42, **42**, 43, 47, **47**; 24th **23**, **A1**(25, 44), 42, **43**, 46; 25th **D1**(28, 45); 40th 5, **D3**(28, 45), 38, **38**, **41**, 42, 43; 45th 17, **D2**(28, 45), **G1**(31, 46), 45

infantry regiments (Army) 40: 9th **C3**(27, 45); 17th 22, **E3**(29, 46), 42; 21st 10; 31st **42**, **47**; 32d **16**, 21

jackets 4–5, **4**, **5**, 6, **7**, **7**, **9**, 15, 16–17, **16**, **17**, 18, 19, **A1–D1**(25–28, 44–45), **F3**(30, 46), **G2**(31, 46–47), **H2**(32, 47), **36**, 38, **38**, 40, **41**, **42**, 45, **45**, 46, **46**, **47**

KATUSA **8**

KMAG **9**

Korean Service Corps 14

Krön, Lt. Col. Jack J. **23**, **47**

lanyards **H3**(32, 47)

leggings **3**, 6, 14, 19, **A2**(25, 44), 42, 46

liners 15, 17, 18, **18**, 20, 21, **21**, 22, **D3**(28, 45), **46**

MacLean, Col. Allan D. **47**

medical companies **G3**(31, 47)

medical equipment **G3**(31, 47), 33, 35, **36**: first-aid kits 6, **24**, 33, 35, **36**, **47**

medical personnel **G3**(31, 47), 33, 36

mess kits 24: canteens/cups 6, **23**, **24**, **A3**(25, 44), 33, **34**, 35–36, **35**, **36**

military police **H3**(32, 47)

mine detectors **G2**(31, 46–47)

mittens 19, **19**, **21**, **22**, **B2**(26, 45), **F1**(30, 46)

mortars 8, 34, 45

nametapes/name tags 5, **9**, **16**, **E3**(29, 46), **G2**(31, 46–47), **H3**(32, 47), **39**, 41–42, **41**, 43

overcoats 20–21, 22, **B3**(26, 45), **47**

pack systems 6, **19**, 24, **A3**(25, 44), **B3**(26, 45), 33, 34, **34**, 35, **36**

parachute systems/paratroopers 34, 43

pistol belts/holsters **D1**(28, 45), **F3–G1**(30–31, 46), **H1–3**(32, 47), 33, 34, 35, **35**, 37, 38, **42**, **47**

pistol/carbine ammunition pouches 7, 36

pistol-magazine pouches **H3**(32, 47), 33, **35**, 36, **47**

pistols/revolvers 16, **F3–G1**(30–31, 46), **H1**(32, 47), 33, 36, **36**, 37

Pollock, Maj. Gen. Edwin A. **7**

ponchos 19, **23**, **24**, 34, 35, **35**, 36, 37

Ranger companies (Army): 3d Airborne 12, **24**, **C2**(27, 45), 42, 43, **47**

rank insignia 39–40: bars 6, **9**, **16**, **19**, **D1**(28, 45), **H1**(32, 47), 38; chevrons 3, 4, 5, 8, 11, 12, **15**, **17**, **24**, **A2**(25, 44), **B1**(26, 44), **E3**(29, 46), **G1–3**(31, 46–47), **H2**(32, 47), 34, 39–40, **39**, **40**, **41**, 40, 43, 45; stars 23, **B2**(26, 45), **F3**(30, 46), 40, **45**, **46**, **47**

recoilless rifles **C3**(27, 45), 34, 45

regimental combat teams (Army): 5th **14**, **F2**(30, 46), 42; 31st 45; 187th (Airborne) **C1**(27, 45), 34, 42, 45

Reilly, Col. William R. **47**

Ridgway, Gen. Matthew B. 11

rifles/carbines 14, 22, 24, **24**, **A1–3**(25, 44), **B1**, **3**(26, 44–45), **C1–2**(27, 45), **D3–E2**(28–29, 45), **F1–2**(30, 46), **G2–3**(31, 46–47), 33, **34**, 34, **36**, **36**, **42**

rocket launchers 34, **36**, 45

Rodriguez, M/Sgt. Clifford R. **45**

scabbards/sheaths 24, **C2**(27, 45), 35

scarves 46

shelter-halves **19**, 24, **A3**(25, 44), 33, 34, **34**, 35

Shepherd, Jr., Gen. Lemeul C. **7**

shirts **3**, 8, **8**, **9**, **9**, 19, **D1**(28, 45), **E3**(29, 46), **F2**(30, 46), **G3**(31, 47), **H2**(32, 47), **36**, **39**, **41**, 45

shoepacs 14, 18, 19, **19**, **B3**(26, 45), **D3**(28, 45), **46**

snow suits 22

submachine guns 18, **H2**(32, 47), 34

sunglasses **H1**(32, 47), 38

suspenders 7, **15**, **23**, 24, **24**, **C2**(27, 45), **D3**(28, 45), 33, 35, **36**, 38, **47**

sweaters 9, **13**, 19, **22**, **36**, 38

tank battalions (Army): 104th **38**

tankers 17, **H2**(32, 47), 38, **38**

tools: axes 34; entrenching tools **24**, **A3**(25, 44), **C3**(27, 45), 33, 34, **36**; picks 34; shovels **23**, 34

trousers 4, 5–6, **5**, 6–7, **7**, 8–9, **8**, **9**, **13**, 15–16, **16**, **18**, 19, **20**, 22, **22**, **23**, **A1–E2**(25–29, 44–46), **F1–G3**(30–31, 46–47), **H2–3**(32, 47), **36**, **38**, **39**, **41**, **43**, 46, **47**

undergarments/underwear 4, 19, 20, 24, **D2**(28, 45), **E2**(29, 46), **G1**(31, 46), 40

US Marine Corps forces: 1st Marine Division **A3**(25, 44), **B3**(26, 45), **E1**(29, 45–46); 1st Provisional Marine Battalion 23, **A2**(25, 44); 5th Marine Regiment 44

vests 19–20